LIFE
IN THESE
UNITED
STATES®

READER'S DIGEST

LIFE
IN THESE
UNITED
STATES®

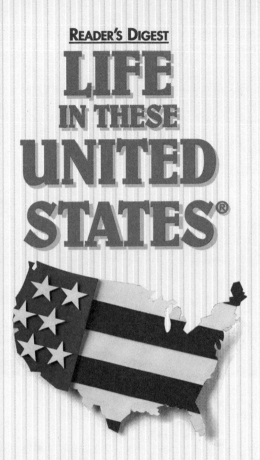

True stories and humorous glimpses from America's most popular magazine

 Reader's Digest

The Reader's Digest Association, Inc.
Pleasantville, N.Y./Montreal

Cover Illustration by Donald Kahn
Illustrations by Donald Kahn, Mike Radencich, Sally Vitsky

Library of Congress Cataloging in Publication Data

   Life in these United States® : true stories and humorous
   glimpses from America's most popular magazine.
       p.   cm.
    ISBN 0-89577-855-6 (pbk.)—ISBN 0-89577-888-2 (hc.)
   1.United States—Social life and customs—20th century—
   Anecdotes. 2.United States—Social life and customs—
   20th century—Humor. I. Reader's Digest.
   E169.L655   1996
   973.92—dc20   95-49496

"Just when I get most depressed . . . something happens to revive my confidence in the goodness of people, the greatness of our country and our common interest in things that are right."

—Andy Rooney, *Not that You Asked . . .*

About This Book

In March 1943, under founder DeWitt Wallace's direction, the first collection of Life in These United States® was published in *Reader's Digest*. In the years that followed, the department became almost synonymous with our magazine. Readers usually turn to our departments first, and Life in These United States® is one of the most popular.

In the front of each issue of *Reader's Digest*, we ask for contributions that are "true, unpublished stories from your own experience, revealing *adult* human nature and providing appealing or humorous sidelights on the American scene."

While our articles aim to touch, inspire, entertain, educate and assist our readers in their lives, Life in These United States® allows readers to tell us *about* those lives. Think of it as our letters-to-the-editor column — true stories about the human experience.

And those stories keep coming. An average of 8000 contributions are sent to the department editor every month. When Americans have something funny to say, they share it with *Reader's Digest*.

So what is a Life in These United States® story? Anything that makes you smile. Anything that reflects the ties that bind us and the day-to-day humor that can be found in the lives we lead as Americans. The best items have a universal appeal. While there are cultural and regional differences between readers, everyone loves stories about situations that we've all experienced.

The stories in Life in These United States® stand the test of time. From its inception, the department has provided a compendium of vignettes about relationships between people and places; stories that make you think about how we look at ourselves and the world; stories that reflect the hustle and bustle of contemporary life as well as stories that recall a simpler time. Stories told through our readers' eyes and in our readers' voices. Stories that might be hilarious, stories that might be poignant, stories that might simply make you smile. Just like life.

—The Editors

CONTENTS

American Traditions

The National Pastimes

Of Home and Hearth

A SENSE OF TIME

THE AMERICAN PAST

During a tour of restored Williamsburg in Virginia, our hostess pointed with pride to portraits of George Washington, Thomas Jefferson and James Madison, our first, third and fourth Presidents. "Why isn't a painting of our second President, John Adams, hung here?" a member of the group asked.

"Because in Williamsburg we only hang Virginians!" the hostess replied.

—CAROL FREESE (Oxford, Pa.) Dec. 1986

Part of our family's Saturday morning routine is a visit to the library where Dorothea, the English-born librarian, always makes it a point to chat with our children. Last summer my three-year-old son, Max, told her that he'd be marching in the village's Fourth of July parade. "I'm going to be Paul Revere," he said proudly.

Dorothea leaned over the counter, looked him in the eye and, in her rich British accent, replied, "Tattletale!"

—THOMAS KOSMAN (West Barnstable, Mass.) July 1991

I was enjoying lunch at an attractive inn on the Delaware River. Thinking that the place must have an interesting background, I asked my waiter, "What's the history behind this inn?"

"I don't know," he said, "but I'll find out."

Several minutes later he returned and whispered in my ear, "I have just discovered the significance of this place. George Washington *never* slept here!"

—RUTH A. HUZZARD (Spring City, Pa.) Sept. 1989

In Philadelphia for the first time, to attend a wedding, we slowed the car almost to a stop to get a good look at Independence Hall. Immediately a policeman waved us to the curb, but instead of accusing us of impeding traffic he said we could park there for 30 minutes while we took the tour inside.

We thanked him but said we were going to a wedding, and had no time. "Take ten minutes," he insisted. "You can see the Liberty Bell and the room where the Declaration of Independence was signed. They've just scraped as many as 20 layers of paint off the walls, and you can see the beautiful grain of the wood paneling."

We still protested we didn't have the time.

"You've got two minutes, haven't you?" he asked, and then added sternly, "Go on in now, or I'll give you a ticket. That's your American heritage in there!"

We took 15 minutes, deeply conscious that on this site was born a nation that had always inspired devotion beyond the call of duty. And we were not too late for the wedding.

—GERTRUDE SCHWEITZER (White Plains, N.Y.) Apr. 1956

The teacher in one of our local grade schools was showing a facsimile of the Declaration of Independence to her pupils. It passed from desk to desk, and finally to Luigi, a first-generation American. The boy studied the document reverently. Then, before passing it on, he gravely added his own signature.

—KATHERINE T. FLOYD (Waterford, Conn.) Nov. 1965

Registration lines for the new college semester were thinning out. The last applicant in the history department was a demure exchange student from Japan. As her adviser, I suggested that she take American history, and I handed her the enormous volume to be used as the text.

She leafed through the pages in wide-eyed dismay. She must have been thinking about the 20 centuries of documented Japanese history, for she asked timidly, "Why, if you please, in so very young country, so very big book?"

—MARY D. BOWMAN (Pineville, La.) Sept. 1969

Last summer, during a Phillies-Mets baseball game, a thunderstorm struck Philadelphia. Everyone ran for shelter—except one young girl, who sprinted out across center field to the flagpole. There she lowered the Stars and Stripes, stuffed it under her coat and, dripping wet, ran to the dugout for cover. All who were present—players, umpires, fans—gave her one of the warmest bursts of applause ever heard in Connie Mack Stadium.

—MURIEL BROTTMAN (Miami Beach, Fla.) July 1968

A few days before the annual air show, we can always expect an interesting variety of aircraft in the skies over the Houston-Pasadena area. One afternoon during rush hour, as I stopped for a red light at a crowded intersection, two Hueys passed overhead.

The driver next to me, a businessman in a well-tailored suit, got out of his BMW to get a better look. Moments later he was joined by another man who had parked his motorcycle on the shoulder. The two men stood in the intersection, their hands raised in silent salute, as the helicopters made their way across our air space.

When the traffic light changed, no one moved. As the Hueys disappeared in the distance, the two men turned to face each other and shook hands without uttering a word. The businessman got back into his BMW, and the biker climbed on his Harley. Only then did the rest of us head home.

—DEBRA LEE THOMAS (Pasadena, Texas) June 1995

A SENSE OF TIME

A World War II tank is on exhibit in Johnston, Iowa. As I was mentally picturing the fierce, destructive action the armored war machine must have encountered, a five-year-old boy charged at the tank, eyes agleam with anticipation.

His mother was alarmed. "Be careful, dear," she called to him. "Don't damage it!"

—J. D. (Keokuk, Iowa) July 1989

During the Gulf War, my sister, Jane, bought a flag and asked her apartment's maintenance man, a Vietnam vet, to install a pole for her. When she offered to pay him, he told her there was no way he could take money for putting up the American flag.

Jane contacted her local newspaper, and they published an article about the incident. The next time she encountered the maintenance man, he told her that everyone he knew had read her story and that she had made him a celebrity. Jane jokingly asked for his autograph.

"I don't have time," the man replied. "I'm too busy setting up American flags."

—CAROL WEBB (Atlanta, Ga.) Nov. 1991

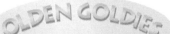

In celebration of the city's 100th anniversary, most of the men in Flint, Mich., started centennial beards. As we stood on a street corner watching the beards go by, the man who possessed the most luxuriant growth stopped to talk.

"How long did it take you to grow that?" he was asked.

"I started on March 21."

"And what does your wife say about it?"

"Oh, she ain't said nothing yet. Come to think of it, she ain't said nothing since March 21."

—JAMES J. HESLING (Flint, Mich.) Jan. 1956

SEASONS

When a colleague's cousin was visiting from Washington, D.C., we took her on several nature walks among our many citrus groves and rolling hills. On one particularly beautiful morning, we were hiking downwind of a large orchard lush with orange and lemon blossoms. The light breeze carried their scent to us in heady waves. The woman reached out her arms and spun around in sheer joy. "This is incredible," she exclaimed. "It smells like a room freshener!"

—JOHN W. GILYARD (North Hollywood, Calif.) May 1991

I had spent the late winter months waiting impatiently for signs of spring. When the first warm, sunny Saturday arrived, I eagerly unlocked the storm door and stepped onto our patio deck. I was pleased by the sight of green sprouts and the sounds of singing birds. More than anything else, I delighted in the sweet aroma of the spring air.

Knocking on the kitchen window, I beckoned to my wife to join me in enjoying the pleasures of the season. She quietly brought me back to earth when she reminded me that I was standing over the dryer vent, inhaling the scent of fabric softener.

—GEORGE G. BUSHER (Glenville, N.Y.) May 1995

While I was grocery-shopping for a Fourth of July party, my supermarket cart bumped one pushed by a Hispanic man. I speak no Spanish, and evidently he spoke no English, so we smiled apologetically at each other.

I looked at the contents of his cart—hot dogs, hamburgers, rolls, potato chips, ketchup and coleslaw—and his eyes followed mine. Then he motioned to my cart, and we burst out laughing. I had selected tortillas, avocados, chili peppers and refried beans.

—JOSEPH C. SPENCER, JR. (Miami, Fla.) July 1993

A SENSE OF TIME

On a beautiful October day, my husband and I were taking a drive through the Georgia mountains. When traffic slowed to a snail's pace, we assumed there was road construction or an accident ahead.

My husband reached for the CB radio and asked, "Can anyone tell me when traffic returns to normal?"

Came the reply: "When the leaves are gone."

—JANETTE F. FORD (Smyrna, Ga.) Oct. 1993

In the fall, my wife and I came from Israel to the United States, where I had accepted a graduate assistantship at New York University. In November we received two letters from the university. The first informed me that it would be appreciated if, as a faculty member, I invited some foreign students to share with us the unique American holiday of Thanksgiving. The second letter informed me that, as a foreign student, I was included in the many offers of hospitality tendered by university and New York City families.

The choice was too difficult for us. So we finally solved it by having Thanksgiving dinner at home—with some *American* students as guests.

—JOEL ADIR (New York, N.Y.) Nov. 1965

FROM THE HEART

My grandfather always had the knack of saying the right thing. One Thanksgiving we explained to my younger brother the custom of breaking the turkey wishbone. Eager to have his wish come true, little Philip was bitterly disappointed when he saw that he held the small end of the bone, while his grandfather had the larger part.

"That's all right, my boy," said his smiling grandfather. "My wish was that you would get yours."

—LINDAANN LOSCHIAVO (New York, N.Y.) Nov. 1983

After Thanksgiving dinner, the adults gathered in the living room to exchange reminiscences, while the children went into the family room to play. Suddenly our hostess noticed that an elderly relative was missing. "Where's Aunt Florence?" she asked.

From across the room came a masculine drawl, "Oh, she's with the kids, bridging the generation gap."

—Florence M. Mortimer (Lakeville, Mich.) Nov. 1985

Knowing that my Jewish co-worker, Morris, had married a Christian girl, I wondered how they would celebrate Christmas. As I approached their house, I could see reflections of a brightly lighted tree and I knew that Morris's new wife had had her way. But Morris had the last word: the tree was topped by a brilliant Star of David.

—Francis Hangarter (Elizabeth, N.J.) Dec. 1968

It was Christmas Day, and we had all gathered for the holiday meal at the home of my husband's parents. After dessert, my mother-in-law left the table and returned carrying a bowl filled with slips of paper. Each adult was instructed to take one. Excited, we did so, wondering what surprise she had thought up for us.

My slip of paper instructed me to dry the dishes; another person was told to wash them. Others had to do pots and pans. Then, with all the parents out of the way, Grandma and Grandpa went into the living room and enjoyed their grandchildren.

—Merna Alexander (Cape May, N.J.) Dec. 1984

All my relatives know that I refold the wrapping paper from my Christmas presents for reuse later. "Auntie," asked one of my young nieces, "why do you save all that paper?"

"I'm doing what's best for the environment," I replied. "So I'm recycling."

"Good thing you didn't ask that question five years ago," my daughter interrupted. "Then she was just plain cheap."

— OKSANNA GUDZ (Royal Oak, Mich.) Jan. 1995

The hostess at a New Year's Eve party was blond, beautiful, buxom—and in a low-cut gown. My husband and another man sat on a sofa watching as she passed the fortune cookies. Bending low, she treated them to quite a spectacular view.

When my husband broke open his cookie, he was convulsed with laughter. Wiping his eyes, he passed his fortune to me. It read: "One good look is worth 10,000 words."

— MRS. PAUL O. SNYDER (Seattle, Wash.) Jan. 1961

EN ROUTE

Last Easter I was scheduled to be co-pilot on an airline flight from Philadelphia to Milwaukee. Before leaving for work, I put a few colored hard-boiled eggs in my pocket, intending to pass them out to the crew. Later that evening, while our plane was cruising along at 14,000 feet, I remembered the eggs. My coat was folded in the overhead rack in the passenger cabin with my cap on top of it. I stepped out of the cockpit into the cabin, put my cap on my head, got my coat down from the rack and was starting to unfold it when a woman in an aisle seat who had been watching me with a somewhat startled expression asked, "Just where do you think you're going?"

— EDMUND KRUMP (LaGrange, Ill.) Apr. 1965

THE SPAN OF A LIFE

Our daughter was filling us in on her date the night before. They had driven to a neighboring city for dinner and a show. When her father asked her where the restaurant was located, she said, "You know, I really can't tell you. I was enjoying the ride, the company and the scenery, and all of a sudden we were there."

"I understand perfectly," her father said. "That's *exactly* how your mother and I arrived at middle age!"

—BERNICE MADDUX (Weatherford, Texas) Feb. 1986

Reminiscing about the past years, my husband and I discussed our children—first steps, kindergarten, Little League and orthodontists. But when we talked about the graduation of our last offspring, I noticed that he suddenly grew very quiet. "Have you regretted any of the years?" I asked.

"Oh, no!" he replied. "I was just wondering what we talked about when we were dating!"

—ETHEL H. BLACKLEDGE (Alton, Ill.) Aug. 1986

Last year my parents attended my mother's 35th high-school reunion. While Mom was reminiscing with some of her class-mates, a man approached my father. "Years ago," he said, "I was madly in love with your wife."

Without missing a beat, Dad replied, "So was I."

—ANN E. HAMILTON (Simi Valley, Calif.) Aug. 1992

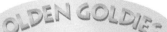

The fact that our 12th-grade English textbook is a generation behind the times became obvious in a recent classroom incident. I was instructing the class in adverbial clauses, and my face turned beet-red as I read this sentence to a room full of giggling seniors: "After I had taken the pill, I was ready for bed."

—MRS. M. W. BAKER (Alexandria, La.) May 1969

High-school sweethearts, my wife and I were soon married and spent the next 27 years raising a family. After our grown children moved out of the house, we experienced an unaccustomed freedom. One morning, when we came home at four, I asked Shirley, "Do you remember the last time we stayed out this late?"

"I think so," she said. "We both got grounded for a month."
—PETER SCHUMACHER (Millville, N.J.) Jan. 1994

At my father-in-law's 35th high-school reunion, the photographer was trying to get everyone to smile simultaneously. All her efforts failed. "Say 'sex'!" she pleaded as a last resort.

"Sex!" the group dutifully chimed in.

Exasperated, the photographer lowered her camera. "Can't you at least say it like you *remember* it?" she asked.
—DINDY ROBINSON (Rome, N.Y.) May 1988

I was having lunch with several thirty-something friends when talk turned to the dismal prospect of our growing older. "Well, judging by my mother," I said, "at least my hearing will improve. Mother can hear my biological clock ticking from 200 miles away."
—SHERRY YATES (Jackson, Tenn.) May 1992

When I discovered my first gray hair I immediately wrote to my parents: "Dear Dad and Mom, You saw my first steps. You might want to experience this with me too." I taped the offending hair to the paper and mailed it.

My father's response, titled "Sonnet to a Hair," began:
It's a trustworthy observation
That nothing can compare
In the process of aging
With finding the first gray hair . . .
He signed off with this observation: "That gray hair you sent us is *not* the first one you gave us!"
—LISA SETTJE (Waterloo, Iowa) June 1989

EN ROUTE

As my parents approached their 50th wedding anniversary, Dad steadfastly refused to have his picture taken. Finally, we used the old argument, "What if something should happen to one of you?" At that, Dad reluctantly agreed to go to the photographer.

On the way home, we did the weekly grocery shopping. Dad was riding in the back seat with all the packages, when we rounded a curve and suddenly hit a cow. The impact was terrific, and when the car stopped, Mom and I turned and screamed simultaneously, "Dad, are you all right?"

From the welter of dust and packages in the back came Dad's disgusted voice: "What difference does it make? We've had our pictures taken!"

—MRS. TOM SHAUERS (Beeler, Kan.) July 1969

I came across a letter that had been written to me 12 years earlier while I was in college. I still fondly remembered the sender—a Shakespeare-quoting, truth-seeking young man—and wrote to his parents, asking where I could contact him.

My letter was returned promptly, with this note scrawled across the bottom: "Our son went on to law school and is a successful attorney. He is active politically, unmarried and, believe it or not, lives at home. *Please come get him!*"

—SANDY CLARK (Monterey, Calif.) Apr. 1989

When the young waitress in the café in my building started waving hello every day, I was flattered. She was at least 15 years younger than I.

One day she waved and beckoned to me. When I strolled over, she asked, "Are you single?"

"Why, yes," I replied, smiling at her broadly.

"So is my mom," she said. "Would you like to meet her?"

—RICK SPIER (Fort Lauderdale, Fla.) Nov. 1992

I had been clearing trees all morning with a friend of mine. When we paused for a much-needed break, a car drove by and the horn was honked at us. We recognized the group of young, single women and waved back.

As they drove away, my friend turned and said, "You really know you're an old married man when you look at a bunch of beautiful young women like that and think to yourself, 'Man, look at all those potential baby-sitters!'"

—GEOFFREY SHELL (Ann Arbor, Mich.) Aug. 1983

 When my husband and I were first married, he moonlighted doing remodeling work in people's homes. One day, we stopped by at the house of an elderly couple he worked for, and the husband joyfully insisted that we join them for some ice cream and cake because it was their 50th anniversary. "Fifty years!" I exclaimed. "That's a long time with one person!"

"It would have been a lot longer without her," the husband replied.

—KAREN JINKS (Houston, Texas) Dec. 1984

Our 88-year-old mother, who had never flown before, was invited by my brother to go with him in his single-engine aircraft to visit me for the day. "I'd love it!" she exclaimed. Later that afternoon I drove them back to the airport and watched as they took off on their return trip.

The next week Mother told my sister's friend about her trip. "My goodness, aren't you brave!" the friend said. "I'm only half your age, and I wouldn't dare fly in a small plane."

"Neither would I, if I were your age," Mother replied with a twinkle in her eye.

—DONALD E. MACDONALD (North Quincy, Mass.) July 1985

Now that they've retired, my mother and father are discussing all aspects of their future. "What will you do if I die before you do?" Dad asked Mom.

After some thought, she said that she'd probably look for a house-sharing situation with three other single or widowed women who might be a little younger than herself, since she is so active for her age. Then Mom asked Dad, "What will you do if I die first?"

He replied, "Probably the same thing."

—JUDY EPSTEIN (Alexandria, Va.) June 1991

A friend and I were eating lunch in a crowded restaurant and overheard a conversation between two women at the next table. "I don't know what to do with her," one woman confided. "She comes and goes, and if I tell her I like to know where she is, she says it's her life and she'll live it as she pleases. She eats junk food and laughs when I point out the benefits of good nutrition."

"Sounds exactly like my daughter," my friend murmured. "Why are teen-agers so impossible?"

"It's a phase they all go through," I replied. Just then the woman's voice came through again.

"I never realized that a seventy-year-old woman could be so impossible," she lamented. "I just don't know *what* I'm going to do with Mother!"

—MARGUERITE MCCLAIN (St. Petersburg, Fla.) Mar. 1984

In conversation, my adult son Larry expressed concern about my future. Confident in my children's love, I announced, "I'm not going to worry about old age. I have four kids, and I'll just spend three months with each one."

"Yes," Larry replied, "but what are you going to do the second year?"

—MARY C. KLINE (Landisville, Pa.) June 1994

On my mother's 65th birthday, my parents and I visited a museum that had special rates for senior citizens and students. Mother and Dad are youthful-looking, and the skeptical ticket agent asked to see their driver's licenses. I had left the business world to return to graduate school, and asked for a student ticket. The agent wanted to check my ID.

"Now *that's* something you don't see every day," an amused bystander said. "Parents trying to prove they're old and the child trying to prove she's young!"

—Carol Hamilton (Berkeley, Calif.) Mar. 1987

A friend was making dolls for her grandchildren. As she was painstakingly finishing a dimpled knee, the phone rang. "Hi, Mom, what are you doing?" came a son's cheery voice.

Removing pins from her mouth, my friend answered, "Making babies."

There was silence at the other end. Then, quietly, "Oh, is Dad home?"

—Thelma Gilmore (St. Paul, Minn.) Dec. 1986

EN ROUTE

I was living in the mountains above Denver when my college buddy, Gary, arrived in his ancient Maserati sports car. He had just driven it from Ohio, and as he pulled into my driveway, the car broke down.

Calls to auto-supply houses and garages in search of replacement parts proved futile. The 1962 model was simply too rare. Responses ranged from "Mas-a-what?" to "You've got to be kidding." One guy just laughed.

I was at the end of the listings in the Yellow Pages when I dialed Victor's Garage.

"Vic," I said, "you're my last hope. Do you carry any parts for a 1962 Maserati?"

There was a long pause. Finally, Victor cleared his throat. "Yes," he replied. "Oil."

—Bob Lacey (Half Moon Bay, Calif.) Apr. 1995

I had just had my 50th birthday and found the decade marker traumatic. When I went to get my driver's license renewed, a very matter-of-fact woman typed out the information, tested my vision, snapped the camera and handed me a laminated card with my picture on it.

"You mean I have to look at this for the next four years?" I jokingly said to her.

"Don't worry about it," she replied. "In four years it'll look good to you."

—NANCY FIRESTONE (Tallmadge, Ohio) Dec. 1987

My wife and I were waiting in line to board a plane for Reno. The gate attendant announced over the loudspeaker: "Anyone under six or over sixty may now board." People with children moved through the line and boarded the plane. A minute later a man came up, obviously over 60.

When my wife and I eventually started to board the plane, we saw that the man who claimed to be over 60 was waiting by the plane's door. My wife asked him why he was standing there. He pointed to the waiting room and said, "My wife is still back there. She wouldn't admit she's over sixty—and she has the boarding passes."

—JOSEPH STRANGIS (Minneapolis, Minn.) Dec. 1983

FROM THE HEART

I am a Baptist, born and raised in Georgia, and my future mother-in-law, who is Jewish, had obvious reservations when I became engaged to her son. However, I knew everything was going to be all right when she gave me a special wedding present.

It was a plaque, on which she had embroidered: "SHALOM, Y'ALL."

—DONNA POLLACK (Aberdeen, N.J.) Dec. 1987

The father of a former high-school acquaintance was telling me about his son's current life. He was married, had two children, earned a handsome salary and had a substantial investment portfolio. The father then asked me, "What have you been doing with *your* life?"

When I told him that I was single, had a modest income, and spent my free time golfing and skiing, he looked indignant.

"Well," he finally said, "I guess growing old is mandatory and growing *up* is optional."

—GARY WRIGHT (Anaconda, Mont.) Dec. 1986

A widow, my friend Casey was dating again at age 62. Once, she was sitting in a golf cart when her escort reached over, patted her leg and said, "Now I suppose you're going to tell me I can look but don't touch."

"Robert," Casey quipped, "at my age you can touch—but don't look!"

—NANCY ALBERT (Mt. Horeb, Wis.) Apr. 1992

Our family held a reunion when my mother was 88 years old, with grandchildren and great-grandchildren attending. The talk turned to honeymoons, and my three daughters began to tell about their trips to Las Vegas, Chicago and Niagara Falls.

One of my daughters turned to my mother. "Gramma, where did you go on *your* honeymoon?" she asked.

Mother never hesitated. "Upstairs!" she said.

—DOROTHY A. ELLIOTT (Wausau, Wis.) Nov. 1988

A neighbor in my Indiana home town has grown old more sweet-ly than anyone I've ever known. Wishing to know the secret of her poise and contentment, I said to her, "I've wondered how it feels to be 85 years old."

Her face lighted up as she answered, "Oh, it's just like Saturday afternoon on the farm, when all the work is done and you're ready for Sunday."

—MRS. DANIEL W. BOYER (Kissimmee, Fla.) Mar. 1967

M other, in her 80s, was gravely ill. My sisters and I took turns sitting at her bedside as she drifted in and out of a coma. Early one morning, while I sat half asleep beside her bed, she nudged me awake. "Dear," she asked, "do you think God forgives us our sins?"

Tears came to my eyes as I bent to reassure her. "Of course he does," I said. "Besides, what have you ever done that you'd need forgiveness?"

Mother closed her eyes. "That," she said, "is none of your business."

—HELEN KENDRICK (Santa Barbara, Calif.) Aug. 1983

A SENSE OF TIME

It was mid-October, and the trees along the Blue Ridge Parkway were ablaze with color. At an overlook, we stood next to a woman who was showing the view to her elderly mother. "Isn't it wonderful of God to take something just before it dies and make it so beautiful?" the daughter commented as she gazed at some falling leaves.

"Wouldn't it be nice if he did that with people?" the mother mused. The younger woman looked at the stooped, white-haired figure beside her.

"Sometimes he does," she answered so softly that she thought no one heard.

—B. G. White (Jacksonville, Fla.) Oct. 1985

OLDEN GOLDIES

My family was apprehensive when, at the ripe old age of 54, I decided to go back to college and get my master's degree. I have been married 30 years, and my two children are in their twenties. On the evening before I registered for my first class, my daughter tossed a paperback book onto my lap. Her sigh indicated that she now felt she had done all she could to prepare me for my new adventure.

The book? Sex and the College Girl.

—Audrey Yonke (Wausau, Wis.) Feb. 1968

FROM HERE TO ETERNITY

At our adult Sunday-school class, the teacher asked us to think of everyday ways in which we could practice our religion. The topic of driving courtesy came up first. "How do you respond to the driver who rudely cuts you off?" the teacher asked.

A woman piped up, "Turn the other fender?"

—SUSAN M. ALLEN (San Jose, Calif.) Aug. 1989

Several days before our annual church picnic, we rowdier members of the congregation presented our minister with a straw golf hat bearing on its band various ornaments such as a beer can, a pair of dice, a shaking hula girl, and other articles loosely classified under the heading of "sin." We told him that if he would wear the hat to the picnic he could expect perfect attendance from us for six months.

He wore it. However, he had made an addition which made it completely acceptable—and put us in our place. He had attached a small sign which read: "Thou Shalt Not."

—KIM TRACY (Abilene, Texas) May 1965

After completing an evangelistic campaign in Nashville, Tennessee, I was driving along a country road on my way to Chattanooga. Hearing singing coming from a small frame building, I realized that I was passing a church where a mid-week prayer service was being conducted. I decided to turn into the churchyard and listen to the service from my car.

When the singing was over the pastor began to pray. He gave a humble but heartfelt plea for divine help in obtaining pews or seats for his congregation. "If it is too much to ask for seats for the younger members, give us at least seats for the older folk," he prayed.

It so happened that in Nashville I had enough extra folding chairs to just about fill this small building, so when the service was over I stepped into the doorway. "Sir," I announced, "you shall have your seats."

The standing congregation turned and looked at me in amazed silence. Then a woman who was apparently more practical than the rest hurried up to me and handed me a pencil and paper. "Excuse me, whoever you are," she said, "but would you mind giving me your *earthly* name and address?"

—THE REV. JERE HENDRICKS (Uriah, Ala.) June 1958

B ecause our former small-town parish was not a wealthy one, our pastor was dependent on parishioners for upkeep and maintenance of the church. Once he asked my husband, Sam, to rewire the confessionals. The only way to reach the wiring was to enter the attic above the altar and crawl over the ceiling by balancing on the rafters. Concerned for my husband's safety, I waited in a pew.

Unbeknown to me, some parishioners were congregating in the vestibule. They paid little attention to me, probably assuming I was praying. Worried about my husband, I looked up toward the ceiling and yelled, "Sam, Sam—are you up there? Did you make it okay?"

There was quite an outburst from the vestibule when Sam's hearty voice echoed down, "Yes, I made it up here just fine!"

—CHRISTINE FODERA (Louisville, Ky.) July 1990

EN ROUTE

After their cars had collided, two women stood arguing about who was at fault. One of them said, "My husband is a minister. What do you think he will say?"

The other woman responded, "My husband isn't a minister. What do you think he will say?"

—WESLY HOLLAND (Nashville, Tenn.) Feb. 1967

In addition to housing an artist colony, our small town is also a haven for retired people. Not long ago, I overheard one senior citizen comment to another, as a group of bizarre hippies went by, "My, I am certainly glad that I don't live in this day and age!"

—C. G. (Carmel, Calif.) Feb. 1968

Every Catholic church in town but one had its Mass schedule posted in front. The exception announced the time weekly bingo started.

I phoned the priest to complain. "My son," he replied, "our parishioners know when we hold Mass, but we have to be sure the Protestants know when we hold bingo."

—JAMES A. DAILY, JR. (Evansville, Ind.) Sept. 1993

After years of planning and saving, the Orthodox synagogue in our town was ready to move to its new temple about a mile away. In keeping with tradition, the moving of the Torahs and other holy scriptures was to be accomplished by a parade through the streets of the town. The parade got under way, led by three rabbis and the cantor, with music supplied by the local drum and bugle corps.

After a brisk half-hour walk, the procession approached the final leg of its journey—up a long hill. The young bandleader called out, "Let's give them some music to help them up the hill," and the drums and bugles struck up the rousing notes of "Onward, Christian Soldiers!" Looking quickly at the rabbis, I saw smiles appear on their faces as they hoisted the heavy Torahs higher, straightened their shoulders, and marched proudly up the hill. Where else but in America!

—L. MILLMAN (Norwich, Conn.) Aug. 1968

At church, our religion instructor rushed in late for class and explained that on her way she had been pulled over by a highway patrol officer.

"How come you're the fastest person on the freeway?" he asked.

"I teach a church class, and I'm late!"

"What's the subject of the lesson?" he inquired.

Looking him in the eye, she replied, "Compassion."

He let her go with a warning.

—STEPHANIE WAGONER (Valencia, Calif.) Oct. 1993

Our daughter was chosen to play the role of Mary in a Christmas pageant. The morning of the first rehearsal we overslept and got her there late. The director wearily dismissed our apologies. "It doesn't matter," he said. "The shepherds have hockey practice and Joseph went ice fishing."

—T. BRADLEY HAYS, JR. (Long Lake, Minn.) Dec. 1985

Our daughter announced that she no longer believed in Santa Claus and flatly refused to leave milk and cookies out for him on Christmas Eve. Upset at losing a four-year tradition, her father tried bribing and cajoling her. Nothing worked.

Later that evening, to my surprise, she walked into the living room carrying a bowl of oatmeal. Her father helped her put the bowl under the tree, next to eight others just like it. "What on earth are you doing?" I asked. "I thought she didn't believe in Santa."

"She doesn't," he said, beaming. "But the reindeer—they're a different story!"

—KAREN DWYER (Williamsville, N.Y.) Dec. 1988

Members of the exercise group at our hospital sported T-shirts containing all kinds of messages. Chuckles broke out, however, when a Catholic priest showed up wearing one from his seminary days.

Across the front was emblazoned: "Expectant Father."

—Dolores Eichman (Mitchell, S.D.) Mar. 1988

A friend of mine, a Sunday-school teacher, attended a church dinner with her husband, who isn't much of a church-goer. The pastor asked each person to stand, introduce himself and describe his contribution to the congregation. As it became apparent to the husband that everyone else was deeply involved, he grew more and more uncomfortable. But when it was his turn to speak, he rose to the occasion. Thinking of his six children, he said, "My name is Dave, and I supply the kids for the Sunday school."

He got a standing ovation.

—Marilyn Meicke (Freehold, N.J.) June 1986

FROM THE HEART

A well-beloved man in our small Southern town was told by his doctor that he had only a few months more to live. He had to give up his job and the last trying weeks were spent in the hospital. After he died, his wife stopped there to settle the bill. She was presented with a statement for $7.50.

"This is someone else's bill," she said to the clerk. "My husband was here for three weeks and had nine blood transfusions, not to mention the services of doctors and nurses."

"No, there is no mistake," the clerk told her gently. "For some time now friends of yours have been dropping by and leaving gifts to be applied on the bill."

—J. Lincoln Moore (Lake City, S.C.) Nov. 1956

My mother writes more checks in April than in any other month. Uncle Sam gets his, her insurance policies all come due and our church holds its annual fund drive. So when the parish priest called regarding Mom's donation, she was quick to jump to the wrong conclusion.

The priest began by saying, "I was wondering if you'd like to reconsider the size of your gift."

"Father," my mother interrupted, "we'd like to be more generous, but you couldn't ask at a worse time."

"I know," the priest continued. "Your check bounced."

—K. J. M. (Shrewsbury, Mass.) Apr. 1992

My cousin, who had just opened his dental practice, was dismayed when his mother told him she was embroidering a Bible verse to hang on the wall of his waiting room. "Mom, you just don't put Bible verses in dentists' offices," he groaned. His mother assured him that he would like it.

He did. The verse his mother had chosen was Psalms 81:10: ". . . open thy mouth wide, and I will fill it."

—MARY ROSE JENSEN (Mobile, Ala.) Dec. 1984

I sell radio pagers, and once was explaining a "beeper" to a minister in our town. As we talked, I realized that he already knew a lot about radios and receivers. He explained that he used to be an electrical engineer. I asked him how he had managed to switch from a highly technical field to theology.

"Well, it's not really such a big change," he commented. "You see, I still deal mostly with Power and Light."

—Huc H. Hauser (SOUTH THOMASTON, MAINE) Jan. 1985

I was visiting with a friend in Utah. One morning we went for a walk in the mountains and came upon an irregular outcropping of rock with a small plateau on top. Rounded boulders, veined in color, rested among the trees, and dark-green plants thrust their way up through the snow to frame a series of waterfalls. "It looks as though it had been professionally landscaped," I gasped.

"It was," my friend replied. Then, seeing my puzzled look, he gestured up toward the top of the peaks and added, "The same guy designed the whole thing."

—E. K. HARLEY (Huntington Beach, Calif.) Jan. 1985

At a church-council dinner, my mother and father were seated at the same table as the pastor. Near the end of the meeting, the latter stood to offer some closing remarks, which became quite long-winded. As he rambled on, he lost his place in his notes for the third time. "Now where was I?" he asked, scratching his beard.

To the delight of audience and speaker alike, my mother spoke up and said, "In conclusion!"

—CYNTHIA LANG SKADAHL (Eau Claire, Wis.) Oct. 1984

As an usher at St. Mark's Lutheran Church in Charlotte, N.C., I had the duty of giving the pastor his cloak after the service to ward off the cold as he greeted parishioners.

Every week, Miss Agnes, a retired schoolteacher and lifetime member of the church, would shake the pastor's hand and eloquently praise the sermon. One Sunday, he jovially questioned her about his sermon's content. Miss Agnes failed the quiz, but refused to let him have the last word.

"I guess I'm like a wicker basket," she said. "If you put me down in a well and bring me up, I don't hold much water, but I feel a whole lot cleaner."

—ROBERT E. KEPHART (Charlotte, N.C.) Apr. 1994

One Sunday our pastor, knowing that many members of the congregation were out of work and broke, put a hundred dollars, in one- and five-dollar bills, into a wicker basket. Explaining that the money was from the church's benevolent fund, he added, "I'm going to do something I have never done before in my ministry." With that, he passed the basket of money to the congregation, urging those in need to take from it, without shame.

They did, but when the basket was returned, it contained $67 more than it had when it started out.

—HARRISON H. HOLTON, SR. (Sacramento, Calif.) May 1984

EN ROUTE

Driving home during a Chicago rush hour, I was in the left-turn lane when a traffic officer waved me on. As I pulled near him, he stopped me and asked why I hadn't signaled. "My turn signal is broken, officer," I meekly replied.

"If you don't mind my sayin' so," he said with a touch of Irish brogue, "the good Lord invented the left arm long before he invented the turn signal."

—TOM SMITH (Whitefish Bay, Wis.) Feb. 1993

I regularly attend an independent Baptist church in the Southeast. One Sunday evening our pastor was giving a sermon on worry. To emphasize the importance of not worrying, he assured the congregation that "ninety percent of the time, the things we worry about never happen."

"So," interjected a self-satisfied voice from the back of the sanctuary, "it works!"

—David Mathews (Snellville, Ga.) July 1995

R ecovering from minor surgery, I shared a hospital room with three other patients. I made friends with the man directly across from me, who had had his appendix removed.

One evening I awoke to see a priest hovering over my new pal, apparently giving him last rites. They spoke softly and then the priest left the room. I got very little sleep that night.

At daybreak I peered over at my friend's bed. It was hauntingly empty. Suddenly he came out of the bathroom, toothbrush in hand. "Good grief, Charlie!" I cried. "That priest who visited you last night darn near scared me to death."

"How do you think I felt?" Charlie responded. "He not only got the wrong guy—but I'm Jewish!"

—Robert M. Quittner (San Diego, Calif.) June 1991

A SENSE OF PLACE

YANKEE SPIRIT

As a Bostonian, I am quite accustomed to books and movies being banned in our city. But the height of propriety came when I read that a local newspaper insists that its writers spell out Boston Redevelopment Authority because the initials make a word not mentioned in polite society.

—CELIA L. PUFFER (Winchester, Mass.) Aug. 1965

On my way through a small New England village, I saw a restful-looking barbershop and decided to stop. Inside, five men were sitting in a row, hands folded, eyes straight ahead. No barber was visible so I spoke to the man nearest me. "Are you waiting for a haircut?" I asked.

"*I* am," he said. Then indicating the others with a sideways jerk of his head, he added, "Don't know about them."

—WHEATLEY MYERS (Boston, Mass.) Dec. 1958

My elderly mother and aunt visited my sister and her husband, Bill, at their summer home in Deer Isle, Maine. Bill took the ladies on a tour of the village. Two lobster men were transferring their catch to a saltwater holding tank, and my aunt—who had never seen a lobster pound—asked what it was. Within earshot of the amused lobster men, Bill suggested to the ladies that they must have heard of "schools of fish." The women nodded.

"Well," said Bill, who is a bit of a wag, "the tank is a kind of lobster kindergarten, where lobsters learn how to enter a lobster trap."

As they moved along, one lobster man turned to the other and said of Bill, "He ain't local, but he'll do."

—BEATRICE BAILEY-FURLONG (Windham, Maine) May 1992

My father, a native New Englander, did his best to instill Yankee thrift in his often extravagant daughters. When I was working as a camp counselor, I gleefully wrote a letter home on a piece of tree bark, pointing out that I had not bought stationery but had made do with the materials at hand.

Once again, however, my father bested me. Carefully separating a layer of the same tree bark, he penned this reply: "Remember, Jean, you can always get along on *half* of what you have."

—JEAN SUMMERVILLE (Punta Gorda, Fla.) Sept. 1987

A friend who was guest speaker at a dinner meeting of Vermont engineers prepared to sit through the usual long-winded introduction. But before he even had time to collect his thoughts, he was being introduced: "You all know we invited Bert Warren up here to talk to us. He's here, and he's going to."

—DR. HAROLD SCHUSTER (Mystic, Conn.) Apr. 1960

EN ROUTE

It happened at Kennedy Airport in New York. My plane from Atlanta arrived late, and I missed the last shuttle to Boston. I indignantly berated the airline clerk about the poor service, complaining that because of the delay I would not get home that night. The clerk explained agreeably that the airline would be happy to pay for a hotel room for me.

Still not satisfied, I told him that it was hours since I'd eaten, and the flight had not been a dinner flight. He handed me a meal ticket, good for whatever I wanted at the terminal restaurant.

Somewhat calmed by now, but still in a complaining mood, I said, "Were it not for your airline, I'd be with my wife tonight." The clerk was quick to reply, "I'm sorry, sir, but we have to draw the line somewhere!"

—S. FERRAGUTO (Lexington, Mass.) May 1968

V acationing in rural Maine, I went into a store to buy a newspaper. Unfamiliar with the regional papers, I asked the shopkeeper if a particular one was a morning or evening edition. "Son," he dryly informed me, "the papers are delivered up here once a day. If you read it in the morning, it's the morning paper, and if you read it in the evening, it's the evening paper."

—ARTHUR GAISSER (Alfred, N.Y.) Mar. 1991

F eeling the winter "blahs," we decided to go away for the weekend and headed toward Maine. Dusk was closing in on the frosty, snow-laden landscape as we pulled into a small gas station near Augusta. "Where can we stay around here?" I asked the elderly proprietor.

"Don't rightly know. Never stayed in a motel," the Mainer said tersely, puffing on his pipe. His young assistant said that a nearby one was nice.

"Do they have any special accommodations?" I asked.

"Well," the old Mainer replied, still puffing on his pipe, "They got an outdoor swimming pool."

—JEFFREY M. WATTS (North Smithfield, R.I.) Jan. 1987

EN ROUTE

I was bicycling on back roads in a small town and stopped at a store to ask directions. The elderly native told me, "Go four miles until you see Jack's big, white farmhouse on the left. The road you want goes off to the right."

After a pause, he added, "Jack's dog will help you choose the right road."

—FRED ARNOLDINK, JR. (Kalamazoo, Mich.) Mar. 1989

We were driving along the New York State Thruway, on our way to Bennington, Vermont. Confused, I stopped and asked a trooper for directions, but his lengthy reply only made things worse. "A Vermonter would have given us clear, brief directions," my New England–bred wife stated.

At the Albany exit, a lean-faced man collected our toll. "Is this the way to Bennington?" I asked.

"Ayeh."

"Thanks. By the way, are you a Vermonter?"

"Ayeh."

As we drove off, my wife said triumphantly, "There, didn't I tell you? When a Vermonter gives directions, they're complete and not at all wordy."

—FRANK P. BIGGS (Hatboro, Pa.) Jan. 1985

We found a charming bed-and-breakfast place nestled in the White Mountains of New Hampshire. Though enchanted, I nonetheless had some questions about the accommodations. "Does the room have its own bath?" I asked.

The proprietor's answer was terse and to the point: "If no one else comes, it does."

—JOSEPH J. SOLTYS (Storrs, Conn.) May 1989

Shortly after moving to the Bangor area from California, I heard two words applied to various local citizens: "Mainer" and "Maine-iac." I asked a native of the state, "What's the difference between the two?"

"A 'Mainah,' " he answered, "is a pehson who likes Maine so much that he decides to stay through a wintah. A 'Maine-iac' is a pehson who is so devoutly in love with Maine that he decides to stay a second wintah."

—WILLIAM E. SMITH (Hampden, Maine) Jan. 1983

Coming from a big city, my friend David wasn't prepared for the approach rural Maine businessmen take toward their customers.

Shortly after David's move there, he rented a rototiller. The store owner showed him how it worked and explained that the charge was not based on how many hours he had it out, but rather how long it was actually used. Looking over the tiller for some kind of meter, David asked, "How will you know how long I've used it?"

With a puzzled look, the owner simply said, "You tell me."

—LOREN MORSE (Molalla, Ore.) Mar. 1992

I work as a courier for an overnight delivery service, and had to deliver a letter to a rural town in Vermont. The address read: "800 Albion Street," but no street of that name appeared on a local map. I took the letter to a store proprietor, who was a salty New Englander. "Cain't be," he said tersely.

"Why not?"

He rubbed his chin, then commented, "If we had an Albion Street, which we don't, it sure as heck wouldn't go to eight hundred!"

—JOHN A. NEWBOLD (Schenectady, N.Y.) Jan. 1986

For the past 12 years, our minister, his wife and two sons have been building a cabin in Maine during their vacations. Each time, they go to a nearby lumberyard for needed items.

Last year, as the proprietor was writing out a sales slip, our minister muttered something about the ever-increasing cost of building

A SENSE OF PLACE

materials. "Why, when I started this project," he said, "sheet rock was one-fifty a sheet, and now it's six."

In a terse Down East twang, the Mainer replied, "Don't work very fast, do ya?'"

—WALTER WAKEFIELD (Rockville, Conn.) Oct. 1986

A friend, a Vermont native, inherited 100 acres of farmland, including several ramshackle old buildings. He had heard that out-of-staters buy old places and rebuild them country style. He put one of the buildings up for sale.

Soon a prospect looked at it and said, "I'm interested. Are you flexible on the price?"

"Ayup," the Vermonter replied. "I could go up."

—R. SCOTT REHART (Brookfield, Vt.) Apr. 1993

I had bought land in a remote area of Maine and built a small cabin. When I had time, I went there to recover from life in the city.

One day, my nearest neighbor, who lived about a mile away, came by on his tractor. He stopped to chat and informed me that he owned 300 acres up beyond me. "It ain't worth much money way back here," he said. "But someday they'll be buildin' houses all over this hill, and you and me will be able to sell at a big price."

He paused and gazed reflectively off into the woods. Then he said fervently, "I hope to hell it don't happen in *my* time!"

—RONALD K. BENOIT (New Gloucester, Maine) May 1984

CITY LIFE

After living in England for several years, I returned to the States and headed for New York City to visit old friends. I had to take a subway uptown, so at the 42nd Street station I stepped up to a token booth, put down 15 cents and said, "One, please." The attendant stared at the money, then at me, then shook his head: "Boy, have *you* been away a long time!"

—MARGARET PLATONOS (Bluff Point, N.Y.) May 1974

All was confusion at the health center. Several diagnostic machines had broken down; technicians were milling around, and doctors were behind schedule seeing patients.

At one point a woman in a purple jogging suit strode purposefully to the front desk. "See here," she declaimed in a loud voice. "I've been waiting since nine o'clock for a 9:15 appointment. It is now 11:30 and, DAMMIT, I WANT MY STRESS TEST!"

—MICHAL SHAPIRO (Flushing, N.Y.) Aug. 1992

A friend and I stayed at a Chicago hotel while attending a convention. Since we weren't used to the big city, we were overly concerned about security. The first night we placed a chair against the door and stacked our luggage on it. To complete the barricade, we put the trash can on top. If an intruder tried to break in, we'd be sure to hear him.

Around 1 A.M. there was a knock on the door. "Who is it?" my friend asked nervously.

"Honey," the woman on the other side yelled, "you left your key in the door."

—BERNIECE B. PHILLIPS (Cuba, Ill.) Apr. 1991

One day I was standing in the aisle of a crowded bus with my arms full of packages. There were many men on board, but no one offered me a seat. However, one more thoughtful "gentleman" tapped me on my shoulder and whispered, "Lady, be on your toes at Chestnut Street. That's where I get off."

—BOBBIE MAE COOLEY (Bowen, Ill.) Apr. 1991

A SENSE OF PLACE

46

My nephew, a New York City subway attendant, tells this story: A girl from the South was having her first experience with the late-afternoon jam at a station in the Bronx. After trying unsuccessfully to board several trains, she approached a guard. "Suh," she said, "Ah've been trying for 15 minutes to get on a train, and it's almost six o'clock and we've got company coming for dinner and Ah've got to bake biscuits—and they will be there at 6:30. So, honest, y'all've got to *do* something!"

The guard paused in astonishment. Then he turned and addressed the mob. "Now listen here, folks," he said. "This young woman's got company coming at 6:30, and she's gotta cook biscuits, so she's gotta get on this next train, see?"

The crowd parted, and the girl marched into the car without brushing a shoulder.

—GENE GREESON (Cleveland, Ohio) July 1978

Contrary to public opinion, New York subway riders are mannerly and do have concern for each other—but you've got to play by the rules. The train I was riding stopped at 49th Street. A middle-aged woman entered, carrying a woolen jacket over her arm. A man sitting near the door quickly got up to offer his seat, then froze in the half-sitting, half-standing position. "I'm sorry," he apologized. "I thought you were carrying a baby." Then he sat down and continued reading his paper.

—JOE LA ZIZZA (Perth Amboy, N.J.) Nov. 1968

On a cold, snowy night in Manhattan, my friend Thea was to pick up her new station wagon. I called to see how she made out. "Did you get the car?" I asked.

"Yes," she replied excitedly. "It's right out in front of our apartment building, and we were just on our way down to sit in it. We're not going to drive it, though."

"Yeah," I replied, "I guess the weather is pretty lousy."

"It's not that," Thea said. "We just don't want to lose our parking space!"

—NEVA SHARON (New York, N.Y.) Jan. 1992

FROM THE HEART

It was a quiet Sunday morning when we parked in front of the Empire State Building, intending to go up to the observation tower. But our two-year-old daughter started acting up. She'd seen the policeman on a horse nearby and she wanted to ride, too. I told my wife to go on in, that I'd stay with the child.

The policeman spoke up. "Give me that baby," he ordered. "I've got six m'self." He reached down, took her from my arms and sat her astride the saddle in front of him. She was in seventh heaven! "Now you go along with your colleen to see the great city," he said. "I'll take care of this darlin' and meet you back here in 40 minutes." Then he slowly clop-clopped down the avenue with our happy youngster.

Amazed at our luck, my wife and I went to admire the view. When we came down, our daughter and her swain were waiting for us. How friendly the big city can be, I thought—a little girl had her heart's desire, an officer had eased his boredom and we had enjoyed the sights unencumbered.

—OREN ARNOLD (Phoenix, Ariz.) Feb. 1965

While I was having lunch at a busy corner in Miami Beach, a large snack-and-sandwich truck drove up to a partially constructed building. Within minutes, chains were slung under the vehicle and a huge crane lifted it—with the driver still in his seat—to the sixth story. There the workmen swarmed over it for their luncheon purchases. Then, ever so gently, the truck was returned to the ground, and the driver casually drove away.

—SAMUEL L. RUSSELL, M.D. (Gloversville, N.Y.) July 1968

On a recent morning in Chicago, harried commuters jammed and shoved their way into our subway train. When it seemed as if every inch of space had been filled, I spied a panic-stricken young man at the car door. Realizing that the train would soon pull away without him, he cried out, "There's room for all 600 of us if we'll just love one another a little!"

The human sea parted, and he slipped onto the train. Despite the crowding and the long ride ahead, we all relaxed a little; the incident had set a new tone of gentleness for the day.

—MAX G. BUNYAN (Miami, Fla.) Aug. 1972

As a student driver in New York City, I was taking the road test for my driver's license. When someone cut me off, I held my temper so I wouldn't look out of control. "You have a lot to learn," said the inspector.

At a red light, the car behind me tapped my bumper. I remained calm while the inspector shook his head. When the light turned, I accelerated, but the car behind sped up and cut me off. That did it! I hit the horn as hard as I could. The inspector turned to me, smiled, and said, "*Now* you're getting the hang of it."

—LINDA CABIBBO (Queens, N.Y.) Mar. 1992

HEARTLAND

A friend who moved from Chicago was surprised at how businesses operate in eastern Wisconsin farm country. When he called the telephone company, which is independent of the Bell System, the woman who answered told my friend that his phone would be installed Tuesday. She changed the day to Wednesday after a voice in the background—obviously her boss's—declared, "Not Tuesday. We're plowing Tuesday."
—JEROME L. SUND (Cleveland, Wis.) May 1977

I was going back to my small hometown in Kansas for a reunion. As I drove into town, I was surprised at the many changes I saw until a hand-printed sign in front of a grocery store made me realize that the old values still existed.

The sign said: "We Accept Visa, MasterCard, Eggs."
—JEANNINE DIXON (Austin, Texas) June 1984

Looking for a new farmhand, we finally settled on an apparently well-qualified young man, who answered our ad from out of state.

The day of arrival he drove his souped-up car to the front gate, quickly surveyed the farm layout, came jauntily up the walk and breezed in. He introduced himself, gave his views on the world situation, suggested a number of farm improvements, and topped it off with a glowing account of his accomplishments to date—all in the span of a few minutes.

As the door closed behind our new hired hand, my visiting brother shook his head slowly and remarked, "I'll say one thing: either your troubles are over, or they've just begun!"
—MRS. NORBERT BORWEGE (Roseland, Mich.) Nov. 1977

D riving across Illinois, we stopped at an old general store. We felt as if we had gone back in time as we walked on the wooden sidewalk up to two benches on the porch. One bench was labeled "Democrat," the other "Republican."

Unaware of the political leanings of the area, my wife sat down on the "Democrat" bench. A farmer in well-worn overalls came out the doorway and glanced briefly at her before continuing down the steps to his truck.

"Don't let folks catch you sittin' there during tomato season!" he called over his shoulder. And drove off.

—STEVE ALLEY (Corona, Calif.) Mar. 1989

A fter my husband, John, and I moved to Michigan from Nebraska, our new friends, proud of their beautiful tree-lined roads, teased us about the Midwest's dull, flat, treeless land. When my parents, Nebraska farmers, visited us, I asked them what they thought about their trip.

"What a boring drive," my father replied. "Once you get to Michigan, there's nothing to see but trees."

—DEBRA MINARICK (Franklin, Tenn.) Sept. 1993

EN ROUTE

Leaving Detroit on a Chicago-bound airliner, I settled back, expecting the usual 50-minute flight. An hour later, the stewardess informed us that because of heavy fog we were in a holding pattern over Chicago.

After two hours of circling, we were asked to fasten our seat belts in preparation for landing. Everyone gave a sigh of relief, and happily followed instructions. But as the plane touched down, the stewardess dealt us the final blow. She announced: "Ladies and gentlemen, I would like to welcome you to Chicago's O'Hare Field. That is what I would like to do. Unfortunately, we're in Indianapolis!"

—PAUL LENNON (Plymouth, Mich.) Sept. 1970

OLDEN GOLDIES

The way of a soldier with a telephone on a weekend furlough is something to watch. One Saturday morning a young GI changed a dollar in a crowded bus terminal, ranged the nickels in rows on the shelf to the left of the telephone in a booth, and placed a cup of coffee and a plate of doughnuts on the shelf to the right.

His first telephone call was lengthy, consisting on his side mainly of repetition of "Gee, honey," and "Sure thing, honey."

A middle-aged civilian waiting for a booth listened, looked over the array of nickels and finally went over to the lunch counter. He came back with a plate of spaghetti and rolls, opened the door of the booth and said kindly, "Here, sonny, you'll be needing dinner in here if all your girls are as big talkers as this one."

—FLORENCE C. BOWLES (Highland Park, Mich.) Jan. 1952

Driving through drought-stricken Iowa on our way home to California several years ago, we stopped in a small town to get something cool to drink. A farmer in a wide straw hat and denims, who was sitting in the shade, remarked, "Yep, the corn's just about ready to dry up and blow away."

"When do you think it might rain?" we asked.

He smiled sagely. "Well, it'll rain when it always rains in Iowa—just before it's too late."

—MRS. TEMPLETON WELCH (Beverly Hills, Calif.) July 1965

After searching for a new home in rural Wisconsin, my wife and I found a beautiful little house on 12 acres. When all the paper work had been completed at the closing, our real-estate agent said, "Well, I guess that's it. Congratulations."

"What about the keys to the house?" I asked. The sellers were dumbfounded. Finally the husband admitted, "I guess we had some keys, but we haven't seen them in years. Welcome to the country."

—ROAK J. PARKER (Amherst, Wis.) May 1994

Driving from Minnesota to Denver, a cousin and her family stopped in South Dakota to spend the night, and began looking for a place to eat. They spotted a restaurant with a sign that said: "Open 24 Hours." But as they approached the front door, the owner emerged and locked it behind him.

"Your sign says you're open twenty-four hours!" my cousin protested.

"But not all in a row," the restaurant owner replied.

—SHERRYL LOEFFLER (Rochester, Minn.) June 1987

After teaching in the Headstart program of the Chippewa Indians in northern Minnesota for two years, I went to a state college nearby for graduate work. One day, four Indian Headstart staff members, who were interested in enrolling in courses at the college, visited me.

I explained the complicated registration procedure as best I could, and the four of them went off to "Step No. 1," on the other side of the campus. A few hours later, I saw my Indian friends and asked how they were doing. "We're registered, finally," said one. "But there sure was a lot of white tape!"

—DAN GARTRELL (Bemidji, Minn.) Nov. 1974

In the mail one day was a thick letter from my son, who had just moved to a very small town in Texas. Eagerly I tore it open. "Hi, Mom," he began. "Just wanted to let you know everything that's been going on around here."

The next four pages of the letter were blank.

—EVELYN TRUXILLO (Gray, La.) June 1987

SOUTHERN BELLS

Our company conducts bus tours for visitors to Atlanta. Most tourists, we find, are fascinated with facts about *Gone With the Wind* author Margaret Mitchell.

On a recent tour, the guide pointed out the apartment building where Mitchell lived when she wrote the famous Civil War novel. Then, as the bus continued on its route, the guide pointed out the spot where Mitchell had been struck by a car, dying a few days later at age 48.

Pondering the tragedy, one woman remarked, "How sad—after all she went through during the war!"

—JERI LEEDY (Marietta, Ga.) Sept. 1992

Attending a family reunion with me in the Deep South, my English bride was a bit apprehensive. She was unfamiliar with a number of things discussed at the gathering, including the eating of frog legs. "What do they taste like?" she asked one of my cousins.

"Well," he explained, "they sort of taste like alligator."

—JOHN W. DOZIER (Manhattan Beach, Calif.) July 1992

Despite the fact that I relocated to Georgia from Michigan 17 years ago, I am constantly reminded of my "Yankee" status. At a gathering, friends and I were discussing our forebears. Proudly I told them, "One of my ancestors was a Hessian during the Revolutionary War, and my great-grandfather was a Union soldier during the Civil War."

There was a silence, and then a native Southerner spoke up. "Didn't anyone in your family fight for the right side?" he asked.

—PAT LANIER (Leesburg, Ga.) June 1989

At a party, one of the men approached a couple who had recently moved to Pittsburgh from the South. Addressing the wife, he asked, "Are you one of those Southerners who are still fighting the Civil War?"

We all silently applauded her answer. With an amused twinkle she replied, "Not unless fired upon, suh."

—MRS. EARL VAN ATTA (Sarasota, Fla.) Apr. 1960

My son Brian teaches school in Exeter, N.H. On a visit home he got together with some of his high-school buddies for a good old North Carolina barbecue.

As Southern hospitality dictates, the waitress brought over a complimentary basket of hush puppies. "You know," said Brian, picking up a hush puppy, "my friends up North wouldn't know what these are."

"Really?" replied one of his pals. "What do hush puppies look like up North?"

—MARY CHRISTISON (Raleigh, N.C.) Sept. 1992

Living on one of the scenic West Virginia runs just off U.S. Route 40, we often see tourists who come to look at our spectacular views. Our house sits on a hill with a lawn that stretches in all directions. One afternoon while I was cutting the grass on one of the slopes I stumbled over a root. The lawnmower flew forward with me holding onto it, and I fell flat on the ground. Stunned by the sudden fall, I was still in a prone position when I heard a child's voice.

"Mama," the child said, "Why is that lady lying down with her lawnmower?"

"Why son," the wretched woman replied, "that's a hillbilly. If they work at all, they always do it the easiest way they can find."

—Mrs. Berny Lanphear (Triadelphia, W. Va.) May 1958

While on vacation in southern Arkansas, I stopped at a roadside stand to buy a watermelon. After discussing the quality of the melons raised around there, I asked the farmer what else that part of the country was good for.

He gazed out over the countryside, and said thoughtfully, "Wal, I reckon this is about the best place in the world to do without something if you ain't got it."

—Warren G. Yandell (Ventress, La.) Jan. 1966

I was recovering from a serious operation in a mountain hospital in Banner Elk, N.C. As the sedative began to wear off and I woke up, I was shocked to find two mountain women, bonnets on, hands folded in their laps, sitting at the foot of my bed in rocking chairs.

"I'm sorry, ladies," I said, "but you must be in the wrong room."

Turning to me, the younger woman said, "Now don't you fret, honey. We ain't going to bother you one bit. Poor Papa died in this room, right in that bed, one year ago today. Me and Mama just want to set here a spell and rock, and think about Papa."

—Marie C. Crawford (Keene, Texas) Oct. 1977

A Sense of Place

When Albert Woolson, sole survivor of the Union forces, died at the age of 109 in 1956, that left the field to the Confederates: William A. Lundy, 108, Crestview, Fla., (since deceased); Walter Williams, 113, Houston, Texas; John Salling, 110, Slant, Va. After hearing the news of Woolson's death, a young lady remarked to me as one Southerner to another, "There now—I knew we'd win in the end!"

—FRANCES JACOB (Rock Hill, S.C.) March 1958

We had stopped at a gas station in the West Virginia mountains when we noticed a battered pickup truck coming rapidly down the hill. As the truck approached, it became evident that the driver wanted to pull into the station but was having trouble slowing down.

We watched helplessly as the vehicle rolled past the pumps and disappeared down an embankment. We ran to help, but the driver had already climbed out, unharmed, and was walking toward us. He pulled out his wallet and drawled, "Reckon I'll have a can of your brake fluid."

—JAMES L. COX (Lynchburg, Va.) Mar. 1974

OLDEN GOLDIES

We received this letter, printed in childish hand, in the group pension department of the large insurance company where we work:

To Whom It May Concern:

My name is Ray Brown. My father's name is Benjamin Brown. Our dog's name is Bridget Brown. My father does not care for our dog Bridget.

My reason for writing this little note is to tell you that Bridget chewed up my father's pension check (enclosed), and if I don't get him another check my father will shoot Bridget.

Please, Sirs, help me out!

As soon as the accounting department quieted down from laughing, we sent another check to Benjamin Brown.

—HARRY C. TERHUNE, JR., AND JOSEPH S. BERGEN
(BERGENFIELD, N.J.) Nov. 1958

BIG SKY COUNTRY

When I first came to live in Montana, I wanted to visit an Indian reservation. The only way for me to get there was to hitchhike.

As I stood by the roadside, a small car stopped and the driver told me to get in. It was a tight squeeze, since the car was occupied by five football-player-size Indians. As we bumped along the road, all wedged together, one of the Indians regarded me thoughtfully for a moment, then grinned and said, "Now you know how Custer felt."

—PAUL BADER (Havre, Mont.) July 1977

A man I know finally accomplished a longtime goal driving the length of the Alcan Highway. In a small Alaska town near the end of his journey, he proudly boasted of his success to a service-station attendant. "I guess that makes me almost a native," he crowed.

"Not hardly," replied the attendant. "A native would've had more sense."

—CAROLYN WRIGHT (Oregon City, Ore.) Nov. 1983

As visitors from Michigan driving across Wyoming, we passed through tiny towns, with population signs of ten or less, consisting of a combination service station, post office and corner store, and maybe a house or two. Usually it would be 50 to 75 miles to the next similar town. Wherever we stopped, the people never seemed too busy to chat.

One Wyomingite, wearing a typical ten-gallon hat, asked us how we liked the state. I said we were impressed with the vastness of its open spaces—and, most of all, by the friendliness of the people.

He chuckled and said, "We ain't jist friendly, ma'am. We're *lonesome!*"

—ARLENE WAGONER (Riverton, Wyo.) Nov. 1977

Last Summer, a New Yorker was visiting for a few days at our small mountain resort in the Utah Rockies. We sat together one night comparing the relative merits of country and city living. I argued that country people were more realistic and down-to-earth; he claimed that out here we were too sheltered from the hard realities of life.

Later, as we walked to our cabins, we paused to gaze at the stars. It was a moonless night, so clear that every star and constellation was visible. "Goodness," exulted my friend, "it's just like a planetarium!"

—RICHARD MENZIES (Price, Utah) Mar. 1969

Although unfamiliar with Alaska's treeless expanses, I was to officiate at one of the checkpoints for the Kuskokwim 300 dog-sled race—a qualifier for the Iditarod. An Inuit workmate showed me the route to the checkpoint two days before the event, indicating frozen bent reeds and other landmarks that would help me find my way.

Early on race day, I drove my four-wheel-drive truck onto the disorienting tundra. I noted the odometer reading, remembering it was 5.2 miles to my destination. By mile three, all the bent reeds looked alike, and by mile six I knew I was in trouble. Suddenly, to my relief, a fur-clad Inuit appeared on his snowmobile. We both gestured a greeting and met at the top of the rise. "Race day," I said, not wanting to admit my confusion.

He nodded, surveyed the horizon, looked at me and responded, "Race day." Then he stared me straight in the eye and asked, "Where the hell are we?"

—BRYAN MURRAY (Salem, Ore.) Dec. 1991

"For lunch," announced the flight attendant on our plane to Denver, "you have a choice of a burrito or a ham-and-cheese croissant." After a few minutes her voice came over the public-address system to inform us: "I'm sorry. We've made an error. Instead of a ham-and-cheese croissant, we have a turkey sandwich." A moment later she told us: "Our apologies. We don't have the burrito. We have a pasta dish."

A passenger across the aisle leaned over to me and said, "Do you think we're still flying to Denver?"

—BOBBI BRANDENBURG (Richmond, Va.) Oct. 1993

Stopping in a small town north of Dallas for gas on a blustery day, I entered the station and remarked to the attendant that it was very windy. He paused, shifted the tobacco in his mouth and stated, "Yep, sure is. That wind is comin' right out of Amarillo and there hain't nothin' twixt here and there 'ceptin' a barbed-wire fence. An *hit's* down."

—JOHN W. MOORE (West Haven, Conn.) Jan. 1982

After moving to Wyoming, our family adjusted to moose in the back yard and to wooden sidewalks along Main Street. However, we hadn't realized the extent to which cattle ranching dominated the town until we observed a cattleman at the grocery store one day. He walked in, surveyed the people in the checkout lines, and went up to a clerk.

"Has my wife gone through the chutes yet?" he asked.

—PAULA STUART (Ogden, Utah) June 1987

As a New Yorker arriving in Dallas for the first time, I was determined to rub elbows with some J. R. Ewing–type Texans. Therefore, when I boarded the airport limousine for the trip to my hotel, I was delighted to see that I would be sitting next to a typical

Texan. He was absolutely perfect from his wide-brimmed, ten-gallon hat to his turquoise-and-silver bolo tie to his lizard-and-calfskin boots.

After a few minutes passed, I decided to open the conversation. "Pardon me," I ventured, "but could you recommend several good restaurants in town?"

"I'd love to help you, lady," he answered in an all-too-familiar nasal tone, "but I'm from Brooklyn."

—J. G. W. (Yonkers, N.Y.) Nov. 1983

I was telling my wife's uncle, a rancher on a small spread, about the wealth of a West Texas ranch we'd visited. Located on its vast acres were large herds and more than half a dozen oil wells. "Yup," replied Uncle Glen. "Those ranches always seem to go better when the cattle have a few oil wells to scratch their backs on."

—HOWARD LARSON (Coppell, Texas) Nov. 1985

I had recently come to this country from India, and was traveling through the West when I spotted an American Indian in full regalia. Stopping the car, I jumped out to take some pictures. When I finished, my subject asked me where I was from.

"India," I said.

"Ah," said he, smiling knowingly. "Columbus was looking for you, but he found *me!*"

—NANDINI KUEHN (Annandale, Minn.) Oct. 1977

A section of Interstate 30 west of Texarkana had deteriorated badly because of heavy traffic and ice storms, and its many potholes had become a source of complaints from drivers.

Before repaving, the highway department filled the holes and cracks with asphalt above the level of the existing pavement. This caused an even rougher ride and more complaints. One trucker was heard to remark, "Nowhere but in Texas could they afford to turn holes over and make bumps out of them."

—EDWARD R. HANNA (Texarkana, Texas) Mar. 1983

I was visiting my company's Dallas office, where the discussion turned to soil conditions in the region. The branch manager said that during dry spells, deep cracks would appear in his front yard.

"You should see the sinkholes in my state of Florida," I said. "A farmer there saw one open under his tractor. He tried to tow the tractor out, but the line snapped. The sinkhole swallowed the tractor, which disappeared from sight.

"So the farmer hired a deep-sea diver," I continued. "After going down 250 feet into the water-soaked hole, though, the diver still hadn't reached the tractor and had to quit."

Just then the branch manager interrupted. "I don't know whether to believe your story," he said, "but I think you'd make one helluva Texan!"

—EARLEY MCFARLAND (Treasure Island, Fla.) Sept. 1993

One night I stopped for coffee at a truck stop in Waco, Texas. Several truck drivers at the counter were trying to outdo one another with highway stories to impress the attractive waitress. After several minutes of statements like "I was doing sixty in high five" and "Smokey didn't stand a chance," a jet from a nearby air base roared overhead. One driver winked at the waitress and said, "It's about time that ole boy got here—we left Dallas together."

—JERRY FITZPATRICK (Van Nuys, Calif.) May 1986

On a road trip through a desolate region of New Mexico, my cousin and I found ourselves 60 miles from town with a nearly empty gas tank. Praying and hoping, we drove on until we reached a small farmhouse standing alone in a vast field. The farmer filled our tank and reluctantly accepted the $20 we offered.

Grateful, I said, "Without your help, two young women might have been stranded tonight. God put you in this spot for a reason."

"Well," replied the farmer, shaking his head and rubbing his neck, "it mighta been a-purpose, but he was mad at me when he done it!"

—ROBIN L. WHEELER (Harvard, Neb.) Apr. 1994

When my brother-in-law was stationed in the Texas Panhandle, my sister, who had lived all her life in Michigan, found the barren landscape very depressing. One hot morning, as she stood at her door looking out over the miles of bleak countryside and longing for the cool green woods of her home state, the postman arrived. Seeing the distant look in her eyes, he stood next to her in silence for a moment. Then, in a tone of awed wonder, he breathed, "Beautiful view, ain't it? And not a tree to spoil the view!"

—FLORENCE W. FREEMAN
(Chicago, Ill.) Jan. 1960

Traveling in Arizona, our family was introduced to a Hopi Indian, who kept the children fascinated with accounts of his tribal customs and beliefs. He also demonstrated a rain dance. It rained heavily that night, and the next day we congratulated him on his success.

The Indian thanked us and then added, "After the dance, I went home and washed my car as a little insurance."

—CHERYL BROOME (Scottsboro, Ala.) Aug. 1978

When we moved to the Texas Panhandle, we left a heavily populated urban area for the wide-open spaces. A few miles from our destination, we drove through Booker—a typical West Texas town with a population of 1,200, and a sign reading: "Booker: Next Nine Exits." Curiosity aroused, we began to count the streets—both dirt and paved—that crossed the two-lane highway.

There were exactly nine.

—RUBY YOUNG (Perryton, Texas) Apr. 1986

When I first moved to New Mexico, the "Land of Enchantment," I admired its desert beauty but missed the greenery of the South. One day the proprietor of a small antique shop was showing me her merchandise, wiping the dust from each item.

"Everything gets dusty here pretty quickly, doesn't it?" I commented.

"That's not dust, honey," she replied. "That's enchantment!"

—RAE STEVENS (Farmington, N.M.) Mar. 1995

In Arizona, I went to see the Hopi Indians perform ceremonial dances. It was a long, lonely drive to the reservation, the last 65 miles of it on a rough road.

After the dances, I returned to my car, only to discover that I had a flat tire. I put on the spare and drove to the only service station on the reservation. "Do you fix flats?" I asked the elderly proprietor.

"Yes," he said.

"How much do you charge?"

Looking at me with a twinkle in his eye, he replied, "What difference does it make?"

—JOHN B. ALEXANDER (Visalia, Calif.) Nov. 1988

Flying into Salt Lake City in a rainstorm, the pilot announced that although our nose wheel was jammed he thought we would be able to land without trouble. As we circled and I saw the emergency trucks waiting below with their lights blinking ominously, I became panicky. The man next to me, however, was calmly reading a newspaper.

In no time at all we had landed safely. My seatmate looked out the window and said, "Well that's a relief."

I wholeheartedly agreed.

"A real relief," he continued. "First rain we've had here in 33 days."

—MARIE MORRISON (Bergenfield, N.J.) May 1960

A fter we moved to Phoenix, I spent long hours in the hot sun trying to acquire a tan. Then a woman in the supermarket asked me if I liked living in Arizona. "How could you tell that I'm not a native?" I inquired.

"You can tell newcomers by their beautiful tans," she replied. "The old-timers have learned to stay inside, *where it's cool.*"
—LOIS M. REED
(Phoenix, Ariz.) Aug. 1985

F reshly graduated from seminary, I was minister at a small church in Texas. The region had been suffering a drought, and one hot afternoon a farmer and I were discussing the weather. "Those look like serious clouds over there," he said, pointing to the southeast.

"You must mean cirrus clouds," I replied, smug with my college education. "Actually, they're probably cumulus clouds."

He eyed me for a moment. "Son," he said, "there's just two kinds of clouds—them that's serious and them that ain't."
—AL HENAGER (Pine Bluff, Ark.) Aug. 1993

A friend of mine, Walt, owned and operated a gas station in the desert town of Hinckley, Utah. As a promotional gimmick, he offered a free road map with each gasoline purchase.

One summer afternoon a man with out-of-state plates rolled in. He put 25 cents' worth of gas into his car and then boldly demanded his free map.

Raising one eyebrow in surprise, Walt growled, "What do you need a map for? I can point as far as you're going."
—WYATT EKINS (Salt Lake City, Utah) July 1995

D owntown Las Vegas traffic was beginning to get heavy as our bus pulled away from its stop. Moments later, we came to a jarring halt. A motorist trying to get into our lane had had his bumper clipped. Two men got out of the car to look over the damage, and our driver joined them outside the open bus door. A hot argument developed. The driver of the car insisted that the bus had been at fault and added, "I have a witness. My friend saw the whole thing." Our driver glanced into his crowded bus and replied with the drawl of a Vegas gambler, "I believe, sir, my full house beats your pair."

—T. K. HARRISON (Bay Village, Ohio) Sept. 1972

A t a restaurant where I was dining in San Francisco's Chinatown, a large Asian family was holding a birthday celebration for their great-grandfather. Everyone was speaking Chinese and bowing in respect to the patriarch.

One relative arranged the group for a family photograph. His instructions, in Chinese, must have approximated, "Move closer," "You two change places" and "Look straight at the camera." Then he appeared to be counting to three, whereupon they all said the magic word, in English: "Cheese!"

—CHARLES B. KIRKENDALL (Sand Point, Idaho) Jan. 1993

EN ROUTE

A state trooper pulled us over for speeding on a deserted road in southern Utah. The road was empty, and he was almost apologetic about writing the ticket. He even complimented us for wearing our seat belts.

At that point, my wife leaned over and said, "Well, officer, when you drive the speeds we do, you've got to wear them."

—CHANCE HUNT (Seattle, Wash.) June 1994

Since we live in Arizona, my sons—ages four and six—are constantly on the lookout for "real cowboys." They were ecstatic when two cowpunchers strode down an aisle in the grocery store. Their rough-and-tumble garb was authentic: dusty jeans, ten-gallon hats and well-worn boots with jangling spurs. "What could they be buying in here?" I wondered out loud. "Probably beer and tobacco."

At the checkout line I saw the cowboys strutting out the door. Tucked under their arms were jumbo-sized boxes of disposable diapers.

—ANNE BUZZARD (Flagstaff, Ariz.) June 1988

HOW'S THE WEATHER?

Born and raised in a large city, I decided to move to a small town in New England for a change from "life in the fast lane." I didn't realize just how laid-back the rural life could be, however, until I heard my first weather forecast on a local television station.

There were no maps or satellite pictures to explain weather patterns. Instead, the forecaster, a kindly older man, cheerfully predicted, "Well, it's rain, rain and more rain! Just how much? Your guess is as good as mine. Good-night, folks."

—LINDA A. STRATE (Whitefield, N.H.) Apr. 1984

My wife and I stopped for lunch in a Nebraska town on our way to California, and I asked the waitress how much snow the area usually got. "About as deep as a meter," she replied. Impressed by her use of the metric system, I asked where she had learned it. She was momentarily baffled, then said, "That's the one I mean," and pointed out the window to the parking meter in front of the restaurant.

—N. A. NORRIS (Grand Marais, Mich.) Feb. 1977

We purchased an old home in northern New York State from two elderly sisters. Winter was fast approaching, and I was concerned about the house's lack of insulation. "If they could live here all those years, so can we!" my husband confidently declared.

One November night the temperature plunged to below zero, and we woke up to find interior walls covered with frost. My husband called the sisters to ask how they had kept the house warm. After a brief conversation, he hung up.

"For the past 30 years," he muttered, "they've gone to *Florida* for the winter."

—LINDA DOBSON (Rainbow Lake, N.Y.) Nov. 1987

When talking long distance to my sister in Minnesota, I have a tendency to brag about the fantastic climate in Southern California. During one conversation, I couldn't resist mentioning a strawberry I had just picked in my garden. "It's almost five inches around," I boasted. "Not bad for December."

There was a pause. Then Sis retorted, "You may be picking strawberries there, but back here we are walking on water."

—PAT KENNON (Escondido, Calif.) Dec. 1977

M y sister Cristine is well-known for her pessimism. With hopes that some relaxation would lift her spirits, the entire family was pleased when she took a vacation in sunnier climes.

Several days later, we received a postcard from her. Printed on one side was a photograph of an idyllic beach baking beneath a golden sun. Next to it, she had written, "Take a few minutes to look at that beautiful sun." We paused to gaze at it, marveling that a few days on the beach had obviously mellowed her. Then we turned the card over. On the back she'd written, "I'm glad you enjoyed looking at the sun for a few moments. That's longer than I have seen it.

"Love, Cristine."

—CHERYL BYNUM (Dearborn Heights, Mich.) May 1995

When I first moved to Florida, the changeable weather fooled me. I read the predictions in the newspaper, listened to radio and TV, but found the statistics confusing—10 percent chance of this, 60 percent that. When a sudden downpour came, chances are I was out in it, and unprepared.

Finally a neighbor, a long-time resident, set me straight. "Just check the morning newspaper after the boy tosses it on the lawn," he said. "When it's wrapped in plastic, prepare for rain. If it has just an elastic band, chance of precipitation are one in a hundred."

—F. HASTINGS (Valparaiso, Fla.) Sept. 1978

One wet, windy weekend I was returning to Juneau, Alaska, on a ferry filled with end-of-the-season visitors. I overheard a frustrated tourist ask a young boy, "Doesn't it *ever* stop raining around here?"

"I don't know," came the reply. "I'm only seven years old."

—PAUL SLETTEN (Juneau, Alaska) Aug. 1983

I had just moved from Mississippi to Idaho, and was feeling apprehensive about the severity of the winters in my new home state. My anxious queries about the weather brought this reply from a native Northwesterner: "Ma'am, we have four seasons here—early winter, midwinter, late winter and *next* winter."

—MARSHA FOLKS (Moscow, Idaho) Dec. 1984

Fed up with the winters of New York State, my wife's sister finally moved to the Pacific Northwest. Her first year was exceptionally mild, even for Oregon. She wrote to her father back home in New York, who had been talking for years of retiring. "Sell the business, Dad," she urged, "and move to Oregon. There's no winter here."

In July, after months of typically cool, wet weather, she sent another letter. "You may as well keep the store, Dad," she wrote. "There's no summer here, either!"

—ROBERT K. HALEY (Woodburn, Ore.) July 1983

Most homeowners in the damp Puget Sound area of Washington State bag their autumn leaves and put them in the trash. So I was puzzled when a neighbor stockpiled leaves in his garage, carefully spreading them out on newspapers.

The mystery was solved on a crisp day in late November. My neighbor, a transplant from the South, brought the now-dry leaves outside, piled them up and lighted a match.

"Now *that's* what burning leaves smell like!" I heard him say nostalgically to his children.

—J. B. (Federal Way, Wash.)

After my wife and I moved from the East Coast to Arizona, one of our concerns was the intense summertime temperatures. Locals always pointed out, "But it's a dry heat."

Our first winter there produced a record rainfall, and flash floods filled even the driest streams. We were listening to the radio as two announcers commented on the unusual weather. "Yes," one retorted, getting in the last word, "but it's a dry rain."
—DAVID GLASER (Tucson, Ariz.) Jan. 1994

A friend who lives in Virginia came to Arizona to visit me. One day, though the temperature was close to the 100-degree mark, we went rock climbing in a local canyon. When we stopped to rest, I realized that the unaccustomed desert heat was taking its toll. My friend was breathing heavily and dripping with perspiration. Trying to encourage him, I said, "It may be hot here but at least there's no humidity."

"There's none in my oven, either," he replied.
—BRIAN K. ARBEITER (Tucson, Ariz.) July 1985

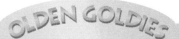

OLDEN GOLDIES

Finding it necessary to take a later plane home, a friend wrote a telegram to his wife explaining the change in the schedule, carefully keeping within the 15-word limit. The telegraph operator, a woman, looked it over and asked him, "Are you married to this lady?"

Startled, he answered that he was.

"Then you'd better add 'love,'" she suggested. "It costs just a nickel more and it's a lot of value for the money."
—JAMES K. BLACKBURN (Santa Ana, Calif.) Mar. 1958

A Park Avenue matron was being complimented on the magnificent display of cactus she has in her apartment window.

"They do well because we take care of them according to nature's plan," she explained. "The important thing is to water them at exactly the right intervals. These plants are from western Texas, and when my husband brought them home we subscribed to a Texas newspaper. We always read it carefully and when the paper says it has just rained in west Texas"—she smiled happily—"*that's* when we water the cactus."

—Dora Davis (Washington, D.C.) Feb. 1972

When I lived in Oklahoma, a series of tornadoes prompted me to call for an estimate on having a storm cellar built. I gave the salesman detailed directions to our rural, back-road location, and he promised to be there by ten o'clock sharp the next morning.

At 11:30, he finally arrived. "You don't need a storm cellar, ma'am," he said. "A tornado could never find this place!"

—Deane Smith (San Marcos, Texas) Mar. 1993

Point Barrow, Alaska, is the closest American continental point to the North Pole. And that just about describes what kind of place it is. One day my father, who was doing a feature story for the Los Angeles *Times* on some of the military stations up that way, was shivering over the pot-belly stove in Point Barrow's general store. It was dead winter, incredibly cold, hundreds of miles of flat, frozen earth from anywhere, and midnight the entire 24 hours.

Suddenly an Eskimo, returning from a tour of duty in the service, burst through the door in a cloud of frost. He threw back the ruff of his snow-white parka, smiled a face full of happiness at the proprietor and bellowed: "Boy, it's great to be home!"

—Steven Sherman (Manhattan Beach, Calif.) Jan. 1966

TRANSPLANTS

Most people in Southern California are from somewhere else, so it was not surprising to hear a young executive complaining, "It's too plastic here. Everything seems artificial. I want to go back to my hometown."

Sympathizing with his nostalgia, I asked where he was from. "Las Vegas," he replied.

—RUTH P. SHAW (Newport Beach, Calif.) Sept. 1976

We had recently moved to the Seattle area from Dallas, and were delighted when one of the church members invited us to dinner after services one Sunday.

"How do you like the scenic Northwest compared with Texas?" our host asked.

"It's nice," I said. "But, you know, Texas is so beautiful that it's where God takes His vacation."

"Yes, that's what I thought when I once drove across Texas," our friend said as he opened the drapes on his window wall, revealing a panorama of towering firs, sparkling lake and majestic mountains. "But this is where He works."

—BENNY L. STEVENS (Kirkland, Wash.) Mar. 1976

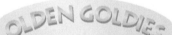

OLDEN GOLDIES

After the Beatle invasion of San Francisco, our teen-age daughter was discussing details of the performance with a friend. "Well, Mary," I heard her say, "You wouldn't have laryngitis today if you'd taken binoculars. You simply can't look through binoculars and scream at the same time!"

—JUANITA F. HACKETT (Walnut Creek, Calif.) Feb. 1965

When we returned to Hawaii after a ten-year absence, we expected the physical changes of growth, but we were curious to see if statehood had changed the carefree island people.

I was reassured one day when, rounding a corner in our quiet neighborhood, I saw a sleek red fire engine, ladder extended. Two husky firemen were happily picking Plumeria blossoms from the tops of the curbside trees, while two others sat below efficiently stringing leis to be worn that night at the Firemen's Ball.

—BETTY R. BUKER (Palo Alto, Calif.) June 1976

When I lived in Missouri, a couple from the city moved to our rural area. Shortly afterward, they bought a ceramic buck, a doe and two fawns and placed the deer family on the front lawn. They were careful to remove the creatures before cutting the grass and dry them after a rain.

We never realized how much the couple liked their little "pets" until the first day of hunting season. All four deer were clad in bright-orange vests.

—KARIN AYRES (Harwood Heights, Ill.) Nov. 1993

Although we were being married in New Hampshire, I wanted to add a touch of my home state, Kansas, to the wedding. My fiancé, explaining this to a friend, said that we were planning to have wheat rather than rice thrown after the ceremony.

Our friend thought for a moment. Then he said solemnly, "It's a good thing she's not from Idaho."

—RHONDA CARLSON (Garden Grove, Calif.) Aug. 1988

AMERICAN TRADITIONS

SMALL TOWN, USA

While visiting Michigan's rural Upper Peninsula, my husband and I became enchanted by the quiet life-style. We drove to the tiny post office to mail a postcard, and when I entered I could hear two men chatting in the back room. As I dropped the card in the slot, they stopped and one of them said, "Uhp! There's a piece of mail."

—MURIEL PEARSON (Farmington Hills, Mich.) Dec. 1993

I live in a farming community. One windy day, after I'd hung my laundry out to dry, I returned to my house just in time to notice that the farmer who rents the neighboring field had begun to plow, sending clouds of dust toward the wet clothes hanging on my line.

Quickly shutting the windows, I hurried outside to retrieve the clothes. But when I got to the line, the roaring plow had disappeared.

Several days later I ran into the farmer and asked him about the incident. With a smile he told me that, yes, he remembered the day. As soon as he saw my clothes on the line and realized which way the wind was blowing, he had decided to plow elsewhere and return to that field later.

Our town has no theaters or fancy restaurants, but we do have good friends and neighbors who care about each other—as well as their laundry.

—MARY LOVE (Farmland, Ind.) July 1995

I had left the hustle and bustle of city life in Southern California for the peace and tranquillity of country living in Kentucky. When winter hit full force, neighbors went out of their way to be friendly. But it wasn't until my car needed some minor maintenance that I got a real taste of country hospitality.

After I paid for an oil change, the garage owner told me he had fixed my broken windshield wiper. Examining my receipt, I mentioned that he had not charged for the repair.

"No, ma'am," he said. "We don't do repair work here."

—JENETTE LITTON (King's Mountain, Ky.) Jan. 1995

Soon after we moved from a large city to a rural town, the hula-hoop craze had a revival. My four-year-old daughter wanted one, and I went to the only toy store in the area. They were out of stock.

At the hardware store, I was telling a sympathetic salesman how disappointed my daughter had been. "We don't sell hula hoops but . . . wait a minute," he said, and disappeared. When he returned, he was carrying plastic tubing. Joining the ends with a coupling, he presented me with a handmade "hoop."

"How much do I owe you?" I asked gratefully.

His answer brought home to me the warmth of small-town living. "Nothing," he said gruffly. "I told you we don't sell hula hoops."

—SANDY HARDIN (Brownsville, Tenn.) May 1989

FROM THE HEART

"Give me a beer an' one for Ole."

"Two malteds and one for Ole."

"Make mine cheese on rye and one for Ole."

It was noon at Rose's Café in a small midwestern town. As we waited for our lunch we heard these strange orders being given at tables all around us.

"Who," we asked our waitress, "is this Ole for whom everybody seems to be ordering something?"

"Ole," she said, "is Viola Dalem. She's in St. Paul being fitted for artificial feet. She stumbled and crawled nearly three miles through the blizzard last year to get help for the 30 school children in her stalled bus. Her feet were so badly frozen that they had to amputate them last spring. Each time a customer requests 'One for Ole' we put the amount of his order in that can beside the cash register and add it to his check—to help pay for Ole's new feet."

"And one for Ole," we said with warm emotion, as we paid our check.

—B. O. B. (Phoenix, Ariz.) Jan. 1950

I got lost in the wild woods of the Cumberland Mountains during a fishing trip last summer, but finally picked up a trail which led me to a group of cabins and a small general store.

"How quiet and peaceful it is in the country," I said to the proprietress. "So different from the mad pace of cities. No people and traffic pushing you around."

"Well," she replied politely, "I wouldn't know whether you're right or not. Fact is, I've never lived in the country—I've always lived right here in town."

—FRANKLIN ESCHER, JR. (Tarrytown, N.Y.) Nov. 1953

After our parents retired, they moved from a busy city in Rhode Island to a small town in Maine. We didn't realize how small the town was until my sister visited the local video store.

She selected a movie and told the clerk that she was going to rent the cassette under her parents' name. The clerk looked at the title and replied, "They already saw that one."

—THERESA COUTCHER SOKOLOWSKI (Warwick, R.I.) July 1995

I am a new resident of Nebraska, just arrived from the East Coast, where populations are usually expressed in the thousands or millions. Therefore, it was quite a change for me when I visited the town of Halsey, population 130.

I noticed a road sign indicating the town of Purdum to be 18 miles north. Anxious to learn as much as possible about my new state, I asked one of the local women the population of Purdum.

She hesitated, obviously wanting to give me the correct figure. After some thought, she slowly remarked, "Well, there's Mr. Purdum and his wife and . . ."

—STEPHEN M. BRATKOVICH (Hastings, Neb.) May 1977

As a former resident of Worthington, Minnesota—population 10,000—I'd grown accustomed to small-town life. But it wasn't until I telephoned a friend to invite him to a bridge game that I realized how small the town actually was.

Thinking I knew his number, I dialed 376-3520. The phone rang. A man answered. "Hello?"

I said, "Ray?"

The man replied, "No, John, this is Merle. Ray's number is 3530."

—JOHN TROTH (Sioux Falls, N.D.) May 1995

Life in a small town has its rewards, but anonymity is not one of them. On a rainy evening not long ago, we had a dinner guest who was quite well-known in the community. During his visit he received a call. Surprised, he took the phone and asked how the caller had been able to find him at our home.

The man on the other end of the line replied, "We saw your umbrella on the front porch."

—PHYLLIS BOGGESS (Shinnston, W.Va.) Feb. 1995

Answering the doorbell one bone-chilling autumn night, I found a candidate for local office standing under a dripping umbrella. "I'm here to offer you a real choice in this year's election," he said. "You can decide whether I don't know enough to come in out of the rain, or if I'm the kind of guy you would send out on a night like this to get a job done."

He got my vote.

—DORIS D. HAMPTON (Niagara Falls, N.Y.) Nov. 1984

The daily hustle of a big city sometimes makes me forget how open and friendly small-town people can be. A last-minute business trip brought me near my parents' home in rural

Wisconsin. It was early in the morning and I phoned, obviously waking up my mother. Cheerfully I said, "Good morning! If I bring some eggs may I have breakfast with you?"

"Yes, of course. Come on over," was the instant response. Then there was a pause. "Who is this?" Mom asked.

—ROLF BOLSTAD (Minneapolis, Minn.)
Sept. 1988

It was the first mild day after a severe cold spell. My mother, who is a teller in a small-town Iowa bank, was trying to make conversation with a customer. She remarked, "It *is* nice to have it above zero again, isn't it?"

The depositor gave my mother an icy stare, then broke into laughter. "For a moment," he said, "I thought you meant my checking account."

—RUSS FELKEY (Wallingford, Iowa) Jan. 1967

Before my husband and I moved to a small town in another state, I phoned its chamber of commerce for information on available housing.

"Hello?" a woman answered.

Thinking I might have gotten the wrong number, I said, "I'm trying to reach the chamber of commerce."

I realized how small the town was when she replied, "I'm sorry. He's not here right now."

—ALISE A. MCCAIN (Jamestown, Ohio) Oct. 1993

The fire department in our small town was holding a pancake breakfast to raise money for equipment. Uncle Ebert, a long-time volunteer, asked a local businessman to buy a ticket. "I don't eat pancakes!" the man told him brusquely.

"And *we* don't start fires," Uncle Ebert shot back.

The businessman bought two tickets.

—RAY TEGNER (Lodi, Wis.) Sept. 1987

Local car-wash businesses were competing for customers. One place posted a sign offering a discount to red cars. The next week, it was blue cars. Soon all car colors had been covered, and I wondered what the owner would do next.

When I drove by a few days later, cars were lined up, but no discount was being offered. A new sign read: "Your Wife Called and Said Not to Forget to Wash the Car."

—AVIS L. NOEL (Augusta, Maine) Jan. 1986

EN ROUTE

Soon after getting his pilot's license, my husband was talking with my Uncle Olson, a farmer with his feet firmly planted in the soil. Again and again Tom urged my uncle to go for a short plane ride, and each time he politely refused.

Pressed for a reason, Uncle Olson finally explained: "Well, it's like this. I never rode in nothin' yet that sooner or later I didn't have to get out and push!"

—KATHY SPILKER (Kings Mountain, N.C.) Nov. 1983

We were building a house on a South Carolina beach. One day I forgot to bring a hammer with me, and stopped by a little country store. Several men were sitting around a potbellied stove, and one rose as I walked in. "Do you have any hammers?" I asked.

"You want to buy one or borrow one?" he drawled.

"Buy one."

"Then I got hammers," he said.

—JOHNNY F. DAGENHARDT (North Myrtle Beach, S.C.) Aug. 1988

Invitations to our daughter's wedding had been sent out, and replies began to come to our home in a small town in New Jersey. Some envelopes were addressed to "Mr. and Mrs.," using the bridegroom's name; others were addressed to the bride's maiden name; still others bore no house number or ZIP code. However, they all found their way to our mailbox.

Then a last-minute letter arrived addressed simply to "Melissa and Don," with no last name and no street address. At the bottom of the envelope a postal employee had penned: "You're pressing your luck!"

—THEODORA A. REMAS (Miami, Fla.) Aug. 1986

When my husband, Tom, was nominated to run for election to the town council, he was not enthusiastic. We live in a rural community of 650 residents, and he knew his election would mean four years of weekly meetings, paper work and headaches. The job also required him to read water meters, help with town mainte-nance and attend every community social function. To top it off, there would be little or no compensation for his time or trouble.

But Tom accepted the nomination. When I asked why, he quoted a former council member who had recently advised him. "In a small town like this," his friend had said, "you don't serve a term—you take a turn."

—KATHIE PALAZZOLO (Clarkston, Utah) Apr. 1995

My 74-year-old neighbor tells many stories about her career as a telegraph operator. The other day I asked her if it wasn't difficult learning all those dots and dashes. "It sure was," she replied. "But it was either that or pick cotton."

—BEA THORPE (Laredo, Texas) Sept. 1983

My farm manager and I were busy mending fences when my housekeeper arrived. Several times during the day, she drove out, returning 45 minutes later. Curious, my manager asked her, "Where do you keep going?"

"Some darn birds built a nest in my car bumper!" she exclaimed. "Every two hours I have to go home because the parents are waiting to feed their young. I wish they'd hurry up and raise those kids!"

—JAMES H. WOODS, JR. (St. Louis, Mo.) May 1986

OLDEN GOLDIES

All the schoolchildren in our community were involved in the Earth Day observances last spring. Even in kindergarten, the significance of the day was explained, and parents were urged to make Earth Day signs or labels which the children could bring to school.

The best sign, by teacher consensus, was one proudly worn on the chest of a five-year-old boy. It testified to his father's awareness of fundamental problems splitting the country. The sign said: "End Pollution—But Keep the Miniskirt!"

—Lawrence S. Sydney (East Northport, N.Y.) Sept. 1970

HOMEGROWN

Pickup trucks pulling horse trailers began to converge at the county fair. An obviously frustrated woman was trying to turn a trailer around, maneuvering it back and forth between a bank on one side of the narrow road and a ditch on the other. Traffic came to a halt.

A man got out of his car, walked up to the window of the truck and said, "Take your time. Everyone has a bad day now and then."

"You think this is bad?" the woman retorted. "I forgot the horse!"

—Lois Lane (Silver City, N.M.) Apr. 1989

It was very early in the morning, and we were on the road trailering horses to a show. Rain was falling as we pulled into a gas station at 5 A.M. to fill up. "Where are you going with those horses?" the man at the next pump queried. "To a show," I answered.

"You horse people must be crazy, going to something like that in this kind of weather," he commented.

"What brings *you* out so early on such a nasty day?" I asked.

"I'm going fishing," the man replied.

—Julie A. Stephens (Lake Villa, Ill.) July 1989

At one church's annual bazaar, the highlight is always a tall-tale contest. A few years back the lies grew wilder and more hilarious as the evening wore on. But the judges' unanimous vote went to my friend, who said in a quiet voice, "In my house, I have two flashlights and two sons—and they all work."

—PAT MOORE (Golden Valley, Minn.) Apr. 1982

A good turnout was on hand for the farmhouse auction and, as is customary, the bidding began with the less valuable items. The auctioneer paused beside a pile of battered pots and pans, and other household articles. He circled the pile slowly as the crowd waited. Suddenly he threw back his head and announced with a wave of his hand, "Folks, this here stuff is like religion—you've got to get it when you don't want it, in order to have it when you need it!"

—LEONARD LINDSTED (Wichita, Kan.) Feb. 1968

I was helping my daughter scrub her pet pig—250 pounds of squealing indignation—in preparation for an upcoming state fair. The phone in the barn rang and I grabbed it. "Hello," I screamed above the earsplitting din. No answer.

"Hello!" I tried again.

"I can hear you," came the amused reply of Jean, the mother of three active preschool boys. "I just thought I'd never hear *anybody* whose kids made more noise than mine when their mother got on the phone."

—MARY HAVENS (Palmer, Alaska) Oct. 1989

Several friends joined me in a visit to a country fair in Maine. We tried the auction first, where the helper brought out the next item up for bid, a small adding machine.

The auctioneer whispered, "Does it work?"

"Ayuh," replied the helper.

"Is it new?" the auctioneer asked.

"Used tuh be."

—BOB BOLSTER (Sudbury, Mass.) July 1993

The annual harvest festival was being held at the county park. In one booth several energetic men were making bean soup in a big iron kettle over an open fire. They put up a sign that read "Bean Soup and Corn Bread—$1.50" and began stirring the beans.

A little later we wandered by the booth again. To our amusement, the $1.50 price had been x-ed out. Underneath was this explanation: "Better Than We Thought—$1.75."

—BARBARA ANDREWS
(Mishawaka, Ind.) Aug. 1989

It was a hot day and we had been holding a yard sale. I stretched out in a lounge chair and unexpectedly dozed off. When I woke up, I heard people laughing and found out that my wife had placed a big sign at my feet while I slept. It read: "Make an Offer."

—JOHN LOCKE (Keene, N.H.) Sept. 1989

It was a beautiful Sunday afternoon in Georgia. After an early dinner, I asked my uncle if he would like to go for a walk and look at a few garage sales down the street. He said a walk would be fine, but that he didn't much care for garage sales. I asked why not, and he answered, "Because if *they* don't want it, *I* don't want it either!"

—LEE HUFSTETLER (Dawsonville, Ga.) Nov. 1983

Every year, our family holds a rummage sale. I have to justify my pricing system to my husband by explaining that no matter how low you mark an item, someone will always want to buy it for less.

At our last sale, one customer proved my point. She approached me, carrying an item that she mistakenly believed was priced at one dollar. "Would you take 75 cents for this?" she asked.

"Sure," I replied, "but it's only marked a quarter."

"Oh," she responded. "Then would you take a dime?"

—JANE MINKEL (Spooner, Wis.) Mar. 1995

FROM THE HEART

In a small shopping center in Oakland, Calif., a barbershop is located near McChesney Grammar School. The barber obviously likes children and has a large number of the active, noisy youngsters as customers.

One early afternoon I went in. The barber was busy with another man so I sat down to wait. The customer was indignantly denouncing children in general and the ones who ran through his hedge on the way home from school in particular. He kept up his tirade, finishing triumphantly with what he would like to do to them.

The barber combed and snipped in silence until the customer had stopped. Then he said gently: "There aren't any kids going home from school. There're Indians on the warpath, Daniel Boones stalking bears, cowboys galloping through the sagebrush after bandits. There's Roy Rogers and Hopalong Cassidy and maybe someone making a winning touchdown."

He whisked the customer's neck and let the chair down. "Don't you remember?"

—K. D. WALLING (Morrow Bay, Calif.) June 1950

PETS AND THEIR PEOPLE

O ur home was on the market, and real-estate agents were constantly bringing by prospective buyers. I am away at work each day, so this was not a problem until my beautiful purebred Persian cat came into heat. Anxious that she remain indoors, I put up a large sign: "Please Do Not Let Cat Out!"

When I returned home that night, this note was posted below my warning: "Another agent must have let your big tomcat out, because he was waiting at the door when I showed your home. I let him back in."

—D. C. PENROSE (Scottsdale, Ariz.) June 1988

W hen she got back to her rural home after participating in an animal-rights march in Washington, D.C., my friend Joan let her pet cat out into the yard. Twenty minutes later she was shocked to find the cat returning with a baby rabbit in its mouth. Removing the rabbit, Joan placed it in a box, grabbed her car keys and headed for the animal shelter.

On the way she accidentally hit a squirrel. She stopped the car, put the squirrel in the box and went on to the shelter.

There, a wildlife worker told Joan that he could do nothing for the animals. "But I'm glad you brought them in," he said. "Now we can feed the owl."

—FRANK MALANDRA (Philadelphia, Pa.) July 1995

M y parents had decided to host two foreign-exchange students, and Mother was filling out the application form. In the space beside "Pets in the home," she wrote: "Three Dobermans—Dolly, 4; Amber, 7; Gypsy, 8. One German-shepherd mix—Sir, 10. Two mutts—Nip, age unknown; Odie, age unknown. Five cats—Spot, 7; Bo, 5; Mama Kitty, 4; Baby Kitty, 1; and Rudy, 1."

Next Mother started to write in the names of the two cockateels. "Don't put the birds down!" Dad interjected.

"Why not?" Mother asked.

"Because they'll think we're eccentric," Dad explained.

—KELLY GORDON MOXLEY (Mountain Rest, S.C.) Oct. 1988

Baby-sitting for a new family, I was hardly inside the door before I was introduced to the aged dachshund.

"If he paws his dish," I was instructed, "give him water. If he scratches at the cupboard, give him dog candy. If he barks at the refrigerator, give him milk. And when he falls asleep on his mattress, be sure to put his cover over him."

"And what about the children?" I inquired. "What time shall I put them to bed?"

"Oh, never mind about them," said the lady of the house. "They'll fall asleep watching television the way they always do."

—LEONORE R. MANDELSON (Park Forest, Ill.) Aug. 1958

Shortly after my husband and I settled in a rural part of Florida, a neighboring farmer gave us a piglet. Thrilled, we named our new pet Peggy and taught her several tricks.

A few weeks later we asked the farmer to take Peggy while we were on vacation. We left her happily playing with the other piglets, but when we returned, we realized all piglets look alike. We didn't think we'd be able to pick out Peggy.

Then my husband yelled, "Sit!" And one little pig sat down.

—SUSAN HORN (Miami, Fla.) Jan. 1995

EN ROUTE

Traveling through South Dakota, I came upon a man and small boy running along the road. When I asked if I could give them a lift, the man replied, "No, thank you. My wife is waiting in the car about a mile up the road."

Noting my perplexed expression, he added, "Have you ever taken a 2,000-mile trip with a 100-mile-limit boy?"

—JOHN J. MCCORMICK (Yakima, Wash.) Nov. 1965

I pulled into a crowded parking lot and rolled down the car windows to make sure my Labrador retriever had fresh air. She was stretched out on the back seat, and I wanted to impress upon her that she *must* remain there. I walked to the curb backward, pointing my finger at the car and saying emphatically, "Now you stay. Do you hear me? Stay!"

The driver of a nearby car gave me a startled look. "I don't know about you, lady," he said incredulously. "But I usually just put *my* car in park."

—Patricia S. Gay (Wellsville, N.Y.) Sept. 1989

I live on a small island off Washington State. All residents must be ferried to a nearby island in order to work, shop and take care of personal business.

My neighbor, Dorothy, has a dog named Pete. One weekend when some vacationers arrived with a female dog in heat, Pete would not stay away from her. Every time Dorothy locked him in the bathroom or the utility room, he managed to crawl out through a window. On Monday morning, she was forced to take him to work with her. Pete protested vigorously as Dorothy pulled him by the leash onto the eight-o'clock ferry.

"I only work half a day, so we'll be coming back on the one o'clock," she explained to the surprised purser. At work, Dorothy locked Pete in the rest room. For a while, he scratched and begged to get out, but soon settled down. At noon, Dorothy unlocked the rest-room door and discovered that he was gone. She searched the office and the neighborhood, but could not find her dog.

At one o'clock, she boarded the ferry in tears. "I can't find Pete anywhere," she told the purser.

"Don't worry," he said brightly. "Pete went home on the eleven-o'clock boat."

—Thelma J. Palmer (Anacortes, Wash.) Feb. 1995

During a trip from New York to Florida our dog, Coquette, became increasingly restless. In desperation we stopped at a drugstore to buy tranquilizers for her. While my husband walked Coquette, I went inside.

I explained to the boy behind the counter what we needed. "The pharmacist will have to get that for you," he said, disappearing into a back room. The boy returned shortly to wait on a woman who had just entered with a collie on a leash.

A few moments later the white-smocked druggist emerged from the back room, walked briskly up to the collie and shoved a capsule down its throat. "There, now," he said to the woman, "your problem is solved. He'll be out like a light in ten minutes."

—NAN COOPER (Elmhurst, N.Y.) Feb. 1967

OLDEN GOLDIES

In a nearby amusement park I stopped to watch several children riding Shetland ponies. The gentle ponies were moving slowly around the inside tracks, and astride them were the very young and the timid. But in the outside track was "Little Miss Hopalong Cassidy" herself. Bent forward in the saddle, she was slapping the pony with the reins and urging him on to a faster and faster gallop. Four times around the track they flew, before she was lifted from the saddle.

"Where did you learn to ride so well?" asked a bystander.

She pushed back her hair, giving us a glimpse of flushed cheeks and shining eyes, and replied, "On the television."

—LOUISE LONGE (North Hollywood, Calif.) Jan. 1950

Much to our dismay, our dog gave birth to 11 puppies. Six weeks later, we put an ad in the local paper: "FREE TO GOOD HOME—11 Adorable Puppies." Response was meager, and at the end of two weeks we still had seven left.

We changed our tactics. The next ad read: "FREE TO GOOD HOME—1 Very Ugly and 6 Very Pretty Puppies." As soon as the paper came out, the phone calls started, all from people who wanted to know if we still had the "ugly" one.

By the end of the next day, we had given the "ugly" puppy away seven times.

—BILLYE SANDERS (Taylor, Texas) Jan. 1985

Before leaving on a two-week trip, my friend took the family dog to his wife's parents, who are Italian. Back home again, the dog turned up her nose at her supper for three days. Desperate, my friend called his in-laws and asked, "Did Pudgy eat while she was with you?"

"No problem," his father-in-law told him. "But remember, that dog is an Italian now. Just warm up two tablespoons of spaghetti sauce and put it on top of her food."

Pudgy ate every bite.

—JANICE A. LARSON (West Valley City, Utah) June 1989

Our puppy, Patton, ate everything he could—remote controls, dish towels, tissue paper. One day I found him slurping up some antifreeze; then I discovered that a spool of thread and a needle were missing. I took the puppy to the veterinarian, who put in an I.V. to flush out the dog's system.

Later, the vet told me he found the needle in Patton's throat. I felt guilty and explained that I tried very hard to take good care of my pet.

"I understand," the vet said consolingly. "He ate the I.V. too."

—SHIREEN RICHARDS (S. Hamilton, Mass.) Apr. 1991

When my family and I travel with our cat, Marilyn, we usually stay at hotels that allow pets. But late one night on a recent road trip, we found ourselves at an establishment that forbade animals. Sneaking Marilyn past the front desk was no problem. However, the next morning when my husband, Murray, put her in a cardboard box and closed the flaps, Marilyn began to meow.

On a crowded elevator, Murray coughed loudly to cover the sound of the cat. Everyone politely ignored the meows coming from the box. When the elevator doors opened before the busy front desk, Murray bravely marched out, praying that the cat would shut up. He needn't have worried. His fellow passengers marched with him, coughing loudly all the way through the lobby and out the door.

—C. E. MUNRO (Mechanicsburg, Pa.) June 1994

My friend Margaret has a dog named Bentley. He barks wildly and runs to the door whenever the doorbell rings. When he hears bath water running, however, he hides under the bed.

To make life easier at his bathtime, Margaret's husband, Bob, goes outside and rings the doorbell. When Bentley comes running, Bob grabs him.

—EVELYN MANNING (Memphis, Tenn.) Apr. 1994

Some motor oil had leaked onto our driveway, and I bought a large bag of absorbent cat-box filler to soak it up. It worked so well that I headed back to the convenience store for another bag to finish the job.

The clerk remembered me. Looking thoughtfully at my purchase, he offered, "Lady, if that were my cat, I'd just put him outside!"

—PATRICIA WARRICK (Fort Bliss, Texas) Sept. 1988

O ur normally sweet Great Dane, Bronnie, has one quirk that we can't explain: she hates United Parcel Service drivers in their brown uniforms. One day I let Bronnie out of the car just as a luckless UPS man walked around the corner of a building. Grabbing her collar, I struggled to keep hold as Bronnie lunged at the visibly shaken man. Trying to ease the situation, I said, "As you can see, she just *loves* UPS men!"

"Don't you feed her anything else?" he responded.

—JOHN S. JOLES (Cheboygan, Mich.) May 1987

M y sister's home was recently burglarized. When the crook was apprehended, and police discovered that he had struck many times in the area, they took him on a drive through the neighborhood to point out the houses he had hit.

Anne, who works for the state criminal justice department, later found out that the burglar had no problem remembering her house. "That's the one," he said, "with the nice little dog that followed me from room to room."

—CHRIS KNAUSS (Easton, Md.) July 1994

M y son Ward owns a shiny green four-wheel-drive truck. He also owns a 110-pound black Labrador named Taylor. On trips, the dog generally sits on a platform behind the driver's seat, resting his huge head on Ward's shoulder as they travel cheek-to-cheek.

Ward did not give this cozy arrangement a second thought until the day he took Taylor with him on a trip to Montana. While listening to his CB radio, Ward overheard one trucker remark to another, "See the little green four-wheeler you're about to pass? When you go by him, take a good look—see if that's a dog driving."

—VERNON WILDES (Concord, Calif.) Mar. 1995

W e were heartbroken when our dog disappeared and, after combing the area, we put an ad in the paper. The morning the ad appeared, the telephone rang and I rushed to answer it.

"I'm calling about your dog," a woman with a rather weak, quavering voice began. I waited eagerly, but she broke off coughing.

Then she cleared her throat several times and apologized. She wasn't feeling well, she explained. As a matter of fact, she hadn't been feeling well since her husband dropped dead three years ago. After that her mother and father had passed on, and recently her sister had contracted a fatal ailment. Her friends weren't doing too well either, she said. She gave me the details of their various illnesses and went on to describe the funerals of several of them.

I tried to be sympathetic. I urged new friendships and suggested that she find a hobby. Then after 30 minutes I hoped it wasn't too soon to get back to the original subject. "About the dog," I said.

"Oh," she replied. "I don't have him. I just thought I'd call to cheer you up."

—DORIS J. JOHNSON (Hopkins, Minn.) Jan. 1960

O ur 96-pound hound dog, an "only child" for nine years, was less than enthusiastic about the arrival of our baby. We had anticipated his discomfort and tried in every way—including formerly forbidden couch privileges and extra treats—to show him he was still a much-loved member of the family.

We thought our efforts were paying off—until the day I took him in the car without the baby for the first time. When I came out of the store, I saw him sitting there, high and mighty, with his big doggie rear pushed into the baby seat.

—G. H. R. (Atlanta, Ga.) Aug. 1990

M y mother often feeds pigeons in the park near her home in Portland, Maine. One day, as she fed the growing flock surrounding her, a man came over to her. "While you're feeding perfectly good bread to the birds," he told Mother angrily, "there are people starving in China."

Mother, never one to back down from a fight, looked him in the eye and said, "I'm sorry, but I can't throw that far!"

—ZINA LETOURNEAU (Biddeford, Maine) Mar. 1994

REAL ESTATE

During the mortgage closing on our summer house, my wife and I were asked to sign documents containing small print. When I asked if I should read it, my attorney replied, "Legally, you should. But here's the bottom line: If you pay your installments on time, there is nothing in there that could harm you. Should you stop paying, however, there is definitely nothing in the small print that can save you."

—MILLORAD DEVIAK (Chevy Chase, Md.) Apr. 1994

It was our first house, and we were avid do-it-yourselfers, full of ambitious plans. We painted and wallpapered, rebuilt rickety steps and repeatedly mopped and patched a leaky basement.

One Sunday night we fell into bed, exhausted from a weekend of projects. When I turned out the bedside lamp, a ghostly silver light flooded the room. "Look," I whispered. "The moon is almost full."

"Don't worry," my husband murmured into his pillow. "We'll empty it in the morning."

—CHERYL HAYNES (Sanbornton, N.H.) May 1984

When a real-estate agency hadn't sold our house, we decided to do it ourselves. I placed ads in the local papers, spray painted a "For Sale" message on a signboard and posted it outside.

When my husband came home that evening, he told me, laughing, that my sign was the most truthful one he had ever seen. Confused, I rushed outside to take a look. In my haste I had printed: "For Sale by Ower."

—MARY ANN BUDNIK (Glenview, Ill.) Aug. 1984

When we decided to sell our house, we nailed "FOR SALE BY OWNER" signs on two trees in our front yard. Before long, the doorbell rang. "How much are you asking for the trees?" a young man asked.

—PAMELA ARNDT (Lake Worth, Fla.) May 1992

After buying our new home, we landscaped it. Since this was my husband's first attempt to plant a lawn, he was careful to do the job right. He prepared the soil, put in a sprinkler system and waited. Finally, after work, on a day when the weather was exactly right, he seeded the lawn, rolled it and watered it—finishing by artificial light because it got so late.

For the next three weeks he watered the lawn daily, often rushing home at noon to run the sprinklers for an hour. He fussed over it, shooed away birds and our cat, and looked for the first blade of grass to peek through. Except for a few weeds, nothing happened.

Then one Saturday morning my husband came in and announced sheepishly, "I just found the sack of grass seed—in the garage."

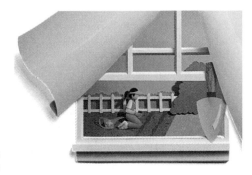

"What in the world did you plant?" I asked.

With a sigh, he replied, "Kitty Litter."

—RUTH N. KOHL
(Redding, Calif.) Apr. 1968

The grounds of our newly purchased home in a rural area had been neglected, and our teen-age son was drafted to help his father clear vast amounts of weeds and overgrowth. As they worked, my husband, proud of his ancestry, remarked happily, "I feel just like a Scottish laird overseeing his estate."

"Yeah," retorted our son. "But the problem is, you have only one serf."

—REBECCA WHITE (Vista, Calif.) Oct. 1983

Dependent on domestic help to run our household, my husband and I have a standard joke concerning the draft they create coming and going so fast. But one recently broke the record.

When the housekeeper I had interviewed the day before turned up for work in the morning, she informed me that she was leaving immediately. On the bus she had read in the paper that the age limit for social security had been lowered to 62, so she was quitting to collect hers. Total time of employment: ten minutes—while she drank a cup of my coffee before taking the bus back.

—MRS. C. J. ROSS (Webster Groves, Mo.) Nov. 1958

One cold night my furnace died, so I went to my parents' house. In the morning, a neighbor called to tell me that my water pipes had burst and flooded my town house and hers. I raced home—and on the way got a speeding ticket.

Then the furnace repairman arrived and told me he didn't think he had the proper fuse but would check in his truck. Meanwhile, the plumber cut holes in my bathroom wall to locate the leak. When the furnace repairman returned, he held aloft a fuse. "I had the right one," he said triumphantly. "This must be your lucky day!"

—CANDACE M. PRESTWICH (Eagle, Idaho) Jan. 1994

EN ROUTE

Driving down the busy highway that goes through the resort town of Myrtle Beach, S.C., my wife and I were stunned by the number of restaurants. One of them got our attention (and our business) with a sign that alerted tourists: "Last Italian restaurant for 100 yards!"

—JOHN A. SWANK (Surfside Beach, S.C.) Apr. 1993

On a Sunday drive with my brother and his wife, my husband and I saw in the distance a house painted bright purple. My brother made several disparaging remarks about it. When we got closer, we noticed this large sign in the front yard: "We don't like the color of your house either."
—OLIVE BRINEY (Raymond, Wash.) Jan. 1993

Whenever my fiancé and I visit relatives in Pennsylvania, we take the turnpike. Visible from the highway is a pasture with a small flock of sheep, and the picturesque tableau is always soothing.

On one trip, we decided to take the exit nearest the farm to get a better view of our favorite piece of scenery. As we neared the field, a woman emerged from the house, picked up two of the sheep and placed them in a different section. They were lawn ornaments.
—A. H. DRZAL (Philadelphia, Pa.) July 1993

Housing in our area is very expensive. My niece and her husband, newlyweds in graduate school, could afford only a used mobile home in a run-down trailer park.

I thought they might be discouraged, but I needn't have worried. On their kitchen wall hung this sampler embroidered by my niece: "Welcome to Our Upwardly Mobile Home."
—GEORGE ROMMEL (Easton, Conn.) July 1994

My husband and I keep the thermostat in our house at a cool 60 degrees. When my mother and sister were visiting us during a sharp cold spell, mice invaded our kitchen. As I was setting traps, I asked my husband, "Do you have any idea why these mice are coming in?"

"Well," I heard my mother whisper to my sister, "you *know* they didn't do it to get warm!"
—KAREN BURGARD (Grass Valley, Calif.) Feb. 1987

REAL ESTATE

Standing in our kitchen, my wife, Marie, and I were surveying the deteriorating condition of the vinyl floor. When I suggested to Marie, a notorious clotheshorse, that each of us forgo buying clothes for a year and spend that money on a new kitchen floor, she recoiled in shock. "No way!" she countered. "You're just hiding behind my skirts!"

—L. PAUL CROWLEY (Provo, Utah) July 1994

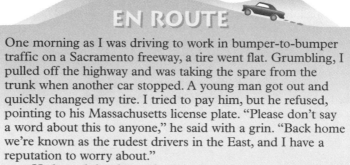

EN ROUTE

One morning as I was driving to work in bumper-to-bumper traffic on a Sacramento freeway, a tire went flat. Grumbling, I pulled off the highway and was taking the spare from the trunk when another car stopped. A young man got out and quickly changed my tire. I tried to pay him, but he refused, pointing to his Massachusetts license plate. "Please don't say a word about this to anyone," he said with a grin. "Back home we're known as the rudest drivers in the East, and I have a reputation to worry about."

He bowed deeply, got back in his car and disappeared in the rush-hour traffic.

—Lynn Vigneault (Sacramento, Calif.) July 1985

We have been building our house for the last five years. One day a carpenter friend came by to tell my husband how to install stairs from the main landing to the second floor. As the men stood in the kitchen talking, I baked a cake and began dinner.

After they wandered into the family room to look at our new home computer, I went by them with a load of laundry, and then proceeded to hang screens. By the time I got outside to mow the lawn, they were walking toward our friend's truck. Ten minutes later the lawn mower quit, and I interrupted their conversation to ask my husband for help.

Our friend looked at my husband sympathetically. "Ain't that just the way it always is, Tom," he moaned. "A man's work is never done!"
—JUDITH A. FRAWLEY (Rochester, Minn.) Sept. 1984

A s a single woman, I had been renting apartments for many years. Finally I purchased a home. On moving day I stood on the back porch as furniture and artifacts were unloaded from the van and carried into the house. Only one kitchen chair remained.

The foreman of the crew brought the chair into the kitchen. As he came back through the doorway, I remarked, "If I were a bride, I would be carried over the threshold into my new home." He turned, picked me up, carried me over the threshold and placed me on the kitchen chair. "There you are, lady," he said.

And without another word, he was gone.
—P. R. LYVENGOODE (Sepulveda, Calif.) Feb. 1984

M y friend Janet, a real-estate agent, was driving around with a new trainee when she spotted a charming little farmhouse with a hand-lettered "For Sale" sign out front.

After briskly introducing herself and her associate to the startled occupant, Janet cruised from room to room, opening closets and cupboards, testing faucets and pointing out where a "new light fixture here and a little paint there" would help. Pleased with her assertiveness, Janet was hopeful that the owner would offer her the listing.

"Ma'am," the man said, "I appreciate the home-improvement tips and all, but I think you read my sign wrong. It says, '*Horse* for Sale.' "
—PAM WILLIAMS (Marietta, Ga.) Feb. 1992

REAL ESTATE

Remodeling the bathroom, the contractor asked my cousin Audrey where on the wall to position the hand-held shower holder. Not sure of the exact height she wanted, Audrey stepped into the tub. At that moment the phone rang. She climbed out and dashed to the phone. "Can I call you back?" she asked her caller. "I'm in the shower with the contractor."

—EDNA MATOLKA (Orlando, Fla.) Mar. 1994

Moving our family, including five small children, into a new suburban home was quite an experience. One morning I was unable to find my five-year-old son's school pants among the packing crates, so I finally sent him off in his good pants, with his promise to be careful.

Later, expecting him home from school, I heard a noise on the front stoop. I was busy feeding the baby, so I called down, "Come on in, honey, and take your pants off."

There was a clattering on the front porch, and when my son did not come in after a few minutes, I went down to see where he was. Instead of my five-year-old son, I found the mail scattered all over the stoop.

—JULIA SULLIVAN (Blacksburg, Va.) Sept. 1983

The man ahead of me at the checkout counter held up a lawn chair. "Young woman," he said to the salesclerk, "do you think this chair will look all right on my lawn?"

"I'm sure it will, sir," she answered.

"It won't look so good that someone will take it?"

"Oh, no, I don't think it will look that good, sir."

"Good," he said. "I'll buy it."

After he had paid and gone, I remarked to the clerk, "Funny old fellow, wasn't he?"

"Not really," she said, smiling. "That was my dad. We borrowed his lawn chair last summer and still haven't returned it."

—WILLIAM L. MOORE (Saline, Mich.) Aug. 1984

We had built our dream house some years ago, and furnished it with quality pieces as we could afford them. Now the delivery truck carrying the last purchase—a new bedroom suite—was pulling into the driveway. "Finally!" I exclaimed, flinging open the front door as the driver walked up to the house. "I've been waiting twelve years for this!"

"Don't blame me, lady," he said. "I just got the order this morning."
—SUSAN TREUTLER (Grand Haven, Mich.) June 1986

We wanted to buy a home in our small midwestern town. As we were walking through a large frame house, a neighbor dropped by to introduce herself as the woman next door who had lived in the same place for 50 years. "You know," she quipped on her way out, "I've lived in a lot of different neighborhoods in the past fifty years—and I've never moved once."
—FLORENCE MELLOTT (Fairfield, Iowa) Sept. 1984

FROM THE HEART

I'm an amateur songwriter and was moaning to my 12-year-old daughter, Karla, about the problems of getting recorded. In short, my joy would be complete to have just one of my works sold and hear it being played on the radio.

After I gave my daughter all the reasons for not attempting this seemingly insurmountable task, she asked, "Dad, do you recall when I was playing Little League baseball? Remember how I'd stand at the plate and get called out on strikes? What did you tell me?"

"I said, 'Karla, if you're going to strike out, strike out swinging!'"

"Dad," she said, "I want you to do the same thing with your music!"
—ANTHONY R. SOCCI (Auburn, N.Y.) Sept. 1983

The dance we were going to was formal. Elegantly dressed, I headed downstairs, picking up in passing a wastebasket that needed to be emptied and a mop that had to be put away.

The doorbell rang. I answered it, still clutching mop and wastebasket. The young man gave me a startled look. "My wife and I were interested in buying a home in this neighborhood," he began, "but if this is the way everyone dresses to clean house, I'm not sure we want to live here."

—HELEN VAN NEST (Youngstown, Ohio) Oct. 1987

OLDEN GOLDIES

Returning from my swim, I noticed a crowd gathering around the pretty girl who had been sun-bathing a short distance up the beach. A second horrified look showed me that, flat on her back and sound asleep, she was unaware that the top of her two-piece suit had come unfastened. She had turned over, but her bra hadn't.

I was debating whether it would be more merciful to waken her immediately or let her sleep on in the hope that the spectators would disperse, when a venerable white-haired gentleman came striding along the shore. He took in the situation and continued on his way.

He had barely passed, however, when he fell to the sand in a fit, writhing convulsively and moaning piteously. The entire crowd swarmed toward him, but nobody knew what to do. Finally someone said he'd call a doctor.

At that point the victim got nimbly to his feet, bowed deeply—like an actor after the final curtain—and walked calmly on his way.

Eyes turned again toward the sleeping girl. Aroused by the commotion, she had disappeared.

—RITA MARSHALL (Lakewood, Calif.) Oct. 1953

My mother always resists our attempts to simplify her life with modern conveniences. She claims it's more relaxing to wash dishes by hand and just as easy to use a knife as a food processor.

Last Christmas, however, we surprised her with a microwave oven. "Look, Mom," I said, "these brownies took only four minutes to bake. Isn't a microwave marvelous?"

"Just what I need," she retorted. "A machine to make me fat faster!"

—CARRIE S. BROWN (San Ramon, Calif.) Dec. 1983

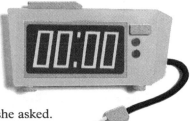

I awoke one morning to discover that the power had gone out for several hours during the night. As I was resetting my alarm clock, a neighbor, whose house bulged with the latest digital appliances, phoned. "Were we without electricity?" she asked.

"Yes. For about three hours."

"I had so many things planned for today," she moaned. "Now I'll have to spend the whole morning reprogramming my kitchen!"

—CAROL L. BECKOWITZ (Peninsula, Ohio) May 1989

Preparing for our move, my husband, Bill, and I held several garage sales to get rid of many items. Soon just a few pieces of furniture and lots of packed boxes remained.

The night after our dining-room set was sold, I was out on the front porch cleaning up while Bill cooked dinner. Then I heard him call out, "Pat, supper's on the floor!"

—PATRICIA SMITH (Punta Gorda, Fla.) Nov. 1993

TO TELL THE TRUTH

Several years ago, I took a course in oil painting. As a beginner, I was delighted to see how much my paintings seemed to improve when they were framed. I even hung a few in my living room. One afternoon, an artist friend was visiting and, as we talked, I saw her glancing furtively at the paintings. Finally, she could contain herself no longer. "Where did you get those pictures?" she asked.

Timidly, I replied, "I did them."

"Oh," she breathed a sigh of relief. "I'm *so* glad you didn't pay money for them!"

—PATRICIA HOUTZ (Rochester, Minn.) July 1969

My dining-room table was set with hand-painted china that I'd recently inherited, so I proudly explained its history to an early arrival at my dinner party. "Every place setting bears the design of a different kind of flower," I said. "No two are alike."

My guest eyed the dishes skeptically. "Well," she replied, "if you don't say anything, perhaps nobody will notice."

—DOROTHY VERHOEVEN (Marietta, Ga.) June 1995

Our bachelor neighbor was shipping some household goods from his parents' home in Connecticut to Texas. The moving van would arrive ahead of him, so my wife agreed to open up his house.

At 4:30 A.M. on the scheduled day, our phone rang. The trucker was outside Houston and needed specific directions. My wife talked to him briefly and crawled back into bed.

"You gave that poor man such a roundabout route that it'll take him an extra hour to get here!" I exclaimed.

"I know," my wife said. "Turn off the light."

—BOB SMITH (Houston, Texas) Jan. 1988

My sister Susan and her husband, Frank, were entertaining for the first time since the birth of their baby. Everything ran smoothly until one of Frank's buddies arrived with his new girlfriend—a woman Susan did not particularly care for.

Susan beckoned her husband upstairs with the excuse that they had to check on the baby. In the privacy of the nursery, she spoke freely of her disdain for the new guest.

When they went downstairs to rejoin the party, they were greeted with an awkward silence—except for the occasional murmurings of the sleeping baby that came from the infant monitor sitting on the table.

—JAYNE HAWORTH (Providence, R.I.) July 1994

A t a dinner party in the home of friends, our host mentioned his high-school alma mater. One of the guests asked him if he had been a student there at the same time as a particular vice principal.

"I sure was!" answered the host. "He's the biggest jerk I've ever met. Did you know him too?"

"Sort of," replied the guest. "My mother married him last Saturday."

—JENNIFER FLANDERS (Mesquite, Texas) Dec. 1993

EN ROUTE

My husband Fred, a state trooper, stopped a motorist for speeding. Instead of signing the ticket and continuing on his way, the driver, who said he knew he had been going over the posted limit, insisted on having a court hearing.

On the appointed day, Fred and the man appeared before the district magistrate. Found guilty, the motorist happily paid his fine. Outside the courtroom, my husband asked him why he had bothered with a hearing.

"I came to this country from Yugoslavia a few years ago," the man explained. "I never had the freedom to ask for a hearing. Now I do."

—ALICE DAY (Du Bois, Pa.) Aug. 1993

We had spent eight years converting an old barn into an impressive home. Pleased with the results, we celebrated with a "house blessing" party. One guest was the old-timer who had helped build the original barn.

Proudly I showed him the stalls, now a spacious bedroom. Then the hayloft with its guest room, bath, master bedroom and—thanks to the addition of 28 windows—spectacular view. "Well, what do you think of the old place now?" I asked.

"Pretty nice," came his measured response. "But you sure ruined a good mule barn!"

—Paul T. Torrigino (Fletcher, N.C.) Oct. 1988

Because of a hasty decision to move into our new home ahead of schedule, it was necessary to leave some furnishings outside for a day while the carpeting was installed. Luckily, I was able to keep an eye on the possessions from the kitchen window.

Late in the afternoon I noticed a garage-sale sleuth examining the furniture. I rushed out to inform her that nothing was for sale, but before I could speak, she said, "I see all the good stuff's been sold."

—NANCY M. HARRISON (Salt Lake City, Utah) Mar. 1991

My dinner party was headed for disaster. One man, an insurance salesman, was monopolizing the conversation with a lengthy account of recent litigation involving himself. Since two other guests were lawyers, I was becoming increasingly uneasy. "In the end," the salesman concluded, "you *know* who got all the money." I cringed. "The lawyers!" he shouted.

There was embarrassed silence at the table. My heart was pounding until the wife of one lawyer said, "Oh, I love a story with a happy ending!"

—JANE GHEGAN (Atlanta, Ga.) May 1992

Hearing glowing stories from friends on the bargains they had found in secondhand stores, I decided to try my luck. Soon I was bringing home attractive outfits purchased at very reasonable prices. At first the idea of used clothing bothered my husband, but he soon got accustomed to it and was proud of my resourcefulness.

My parents came to visit us, and I showed off my latest find, which had cost only a few dollars. My husband put his arm around me and declared happily, "Nothing but the second best for my wife."
—DOROTHY G. BUTO (Fountain Valley, Calif.) Apr. 1984

After a long, exhausting day, a friend of mine headed home. On the road, he passed an elderly woman who was standing by a car with a flat tire. His conscience got the better of him; *if* that were *his* mother, he thought, he would want someone to help her. With a tired sigh, he turned around and drove back.

Just as he reached the stranded woman, a truck pulled up and a burly farmer got out. "Kinda reminds you of *your* mom, too?" the man asked as the two of them pitched in together to change the tire.
—KATHERINE L. HOGUE (Cincinnati, Ohio) June 1987

My husband had a favorite pair of jeans that he refused to throw out when the seat became worn. I sewed some colorful patches on the rear, and he continued to wear them.

One summer day we were traveling through New England and stopped at a rural grocery store. An elderly man was sitting on the porch, lazily rocking in the heat. My husband's patched jeans did not escape his notice. "Well, sonny," he called out, "it's easy to see where you do all your work from!"
—TRUDY WHYNOTT (Acme, Wash.) July 1988

GOOD NEIGHBORS

Not long ago one of my sisters sent away for a copy of her birth certificate. When it arrived and she showed it to the rest of the family, we all burst out laughing. It brought back one of the most delightful memories of our childhood—the rivalry between our father and his best friend, who was our family doctor.

Both men were incorrigible practical jokers who would go to any lengths to play a trick on one another. I can remember many an evening when we listened wide-eyed as Papa plotted his newest scheme to foil the doctor. He and his friend have been dead many years, but as we looked at the certificate we thought of how exasperated he would have been to see that Doctor had had the last laugh. For in the space following the words "Father's Occupation," was written "Hog Thief."

—ANNE MORGAN (Pasadena, Texas) June 1958

Within minutes, everyone in the neighborhood had heard the searing words: "Killed in Vietnam." A wave of gloom spread through the street, where not so many months earlier the man—then just a boy—had walked self-consciously in his new uniform, smiling with the awkward pride of a young soldier. Neighbors offered his parents feeble words of sympathy, but no one really knew what to do or say.

Next day, the answer came. When the soft light of early morning reached the lawn of the soldier's home, it fell upon an American flag placed there by his anguished parents. It fluttered proudly in the breeze. As one mind, the neighborhood recognized the gesture, and in rapid succession flags went up at house after house. Soon the street was two streaming columns of red, white and blue—a mass display of sympathy and recognition for a sacrifice too great to capture in words.

—S. H. McGUIRE (Lakewood, Ohio) May 1969

When my husband and I moved into our new home, the neighborhood children who were watching the van came in and asked where my children were. I explained that there were none in our family.

A few days later one of the little boys came to call. "I have something for you," he said shyly as he handed me a pink-and-blue book. "My mother's going to have a baby, and she gave me this book which tells you where babies come from. I thought you and your husband would like to read it."

—DOROTHY O. REA (Provo, Utah) June 1960

My neighbors planned their daughter's wedding hastily because she and her Navy groom would soon be transferred overseas. Flowers, minister and cake were arranged for the ceremony in her parents' home. But then the invitations arrived from the printer with the wrong house number—717 instead of 719.

Since it was too late to rectify the error, the bride came up with the next-best solution. She phoned the family who lived at 717. The morning of the big day, screwdriver in hand, she raced to their home and switched the house numbers.

—JANNA GAGE (Mount Vernon, Wash.) Jan. 1994

We had moved to North Dakota from Los Angeles, and my wife had begun teaching in a two-room rural school. One February morning, with the temperature at 30 below, someone from the school phoned to tell me my wife hadn't arrived. Frantic with worry, I contacted the state police.

Ten minutes later, my wife called. She had been stuck only a short while when a farmer had arrived with his tractor and pulled her from a snowdrift. As she thanked him, she asked how he had known that she needed help.

"Only the school bus and you go by here," he replied. "Bus did, you didn't. Missed you and went looking."

—ALFRED A. BELTRAN (Bismarck, N.D.) Feb. 1985

New York's Third Avenue was almost deserted when I went out to get an evening paper. I was startled when the phone in a corner booth jangled urgently as I passed, but curious enough to pick it up. A voice asked if this was 30th Street and Third Avenue. When I assured the man it was, he directed my attention to some power-company gear in the street near the booth, and asked if I saw a yellow warning light there. I told him it wasn't lighted. In tones of anguish he admitted he'd forgotten to light it.

"Look, buddy," he pleaded. "I'm all the way up in the Bronx. Do you suppose you could turn on that light? I sure would appreciate it."

The apparatus looked intricate, but I agreed to try. Following his instructions, I found an ominous-looking black box with a conspicuous warning against touching the switch. Gingerly I pulled it toward me and gasped with relief as the warning flash emblazoned the street. "It's lit! It's lit!" I shouted into the phone. My cohort gave a whoop of delight, and we bade each other a hearty good-night.

—ALLEN ANDREWS (New York, N.Y.) Dec. 1965

When my husband and I were first married, we spent much of our free time grilling dinner on our patio and speculating about the other couples living in our condominium complex. We named them all: the Activity Fans ran about in sweat pants and sneakers, the Newlyweds strolled arm in arm, the Shoppers never came home without packages, and the Carryouts had Chinese food delivered every other night.

One morning Mrs. Newlywed knocked on our door, explaining that she had locked herself out of her condo and needed to phone her husband. She told him she was calling from a neighbor's and asked him to come home and let her in. He must have asked her which neighbor, because she glanced at me and shielded the receiver with her hand. "You know," she whispered into the phone, "the Barbecuers!"

—LAURA BETHEA (Centreville, Va.) Aug. 1994

L ooking through my cookbooks for a new dessert to try, I came across a recipe with the intriguing name "Better Than Sex Cake." I baked it and took two pieces to my next-door neighbors. After telling them the cake's name, I laughingly added, "Decide for yourselves."

The next morning this note appeared in their bedroom window: "Please send more cake. We can't make up our minds."

—KAREN L. GIEFER (Downers Grove, Ill.) Feb. 1988

T he volunteer fire department was fighting the blaze engulfing my cousin's barn. As he watched, he dialed his insurance company on his portable phone, but there was no answer. "How come my agent is never there when I need him?" he asked in frustration.

One of the firefighters tapped him on the shoulder. "That's because I'm right here, putting out the fire," responded the agent.

—JULIA CAMPBELL (Hurricane, Utah) Feb. 1993

O utside a department store, I noticed a young man with a baby in one arm and a three-year-old in tow, struggling to get through the door. A well-dressed woman swung it open for him. "Thank you," the man said. "I guess chivalry is not dead."

"No," the woman replied. "It just changed hands."

—EARL EVES (Las Vegas, Nev.) Jan. 1989

We were staying at a resort in New Hampshire and became friendly with the handyman. "My neighbor has a nice little cottage for sale, case you're interested," he told us.

Despite its run-down appearance, we fell in love with the place and bought it "as is." The day we moved in, our friend dropped by. "You got a good buy," he admitted. "Cottage needs some work though. Roof leaks, plumbing's shot and the well runs dry in the summer."

Dismayed, I retorted, "Why didn't you tell us that before we bought it?"

"Weren't neighbors then," he replied.

—ROBERT F. PETERSON (Howell, N.J.) Feb. 1989

While in a Maine country store, I reached into my pocket for the $20 bill I had put there, but it was gone. I quickly retraced my steps to the parking area.

"Lose something?" asked the driver of a car near mine.

"A $20 bill," I replied.

"Here it is," he said, handing me the money.

Elated, I asked, "What can I do for you in return?"

"Nothing," answered the driver's companion as they started to drive off. "Glad to do it."

Then the two good Samaritans backed their car up. "There is something you can do for us," the driver said. "When you go home and talk about this, please tell everybody we're from New York City."

—JEAN BAUER FISLER (Bethesda, Md.) Nov. 1991

A s a daily warrior on Route 95 from the Virginia suburbs, I've witnessed many random acts of kindness delivered with local flair. On a recent morning, I noticed a commuter standing in the pouring rain beside his disabled vehicle, helplessly watching the procession of cars pass him by. Suddenly one small car, already packed with four passengers, swerved close to the drenched man. Down rolled the window and from it emerged a well-used yet functional umbrella. The still-stranded but grateful man accepted the gift, waved his thanks, and the car continued on its way.

—DIANN TENNANT WOHLLEB (Occoquan, Va.) Aug. 1994

EN ROUTE

The rush-hour commute to my job in Atlanta is often nerve-racking, so I make it a point to be a careful and considerate motorist. One morning, as I occupied the left lane of Interstate 85, an 18-wheel truck was on my right. As we approached an entrance ramp, a compact car pulled slowly onto the highway and into the path of the truck.

I reduced my speed, allowing the truck driver into the left lane ahead of me. After passing the slow-moving car, the trucker moved back into the right lane, and I resumed my speed.

My day was made when, in response to a toot of its horn, I glanced back at the truck. The driver was holding a rose against the window. Attached to it was a large placard that read: "This bud's for you!"

—MARLENE WEBER (Sharpsburg, Ga.) July 1994

M y father-in-law, Bud, is a retired Nebraska cowboy, with a rugged character and quiet strength. I didn't realize how quiet, however, until recently. As Bud was driving down a country road, a neighbor's truck passed him, heading in the opposite direction. Both men immediately stopped their pickups and backed up until the trucks were side by side.

That accomplished, they nodded to each other—and drove on.
—LINDA HUNTINGTON (Grand Rapids, Minn.) Mar. 1988

OLDEN GOLDIES

The first time President Eisenhower came to see his brother Milton in the little town of State College, Pa., all the residents were tremendously excited. We eagerly read details of the approaching visit in the local papers. Among other things, we learned that, although the town has only a freight shuttle railroad line, the President's train was going to be routed over it and would remain on the siding during his stay.

For some reason, this bit of information seemed to thrill the neighborhood children more than anything else. In fact it was quite obvious that they were more interested in the train than they were in the President himself, and no one could understand why.

When the big day came, everybody gathered at the railroad siding. The President arrived, and we all had a chance to see him before he was driven to his brother's house. Then the adults left. But the children kept on standing, staring at the empty train. It was at least two hours before our own young daughter came slowly in the door.

"I wanted to see the Presidential seal," she said sadly.

"You must have seen it," we said. "It was right on the train."

She shook her head. "That's what our teacher said. But none of us saw it." She was thoughtful for a moment. Then she looked more cheerful. "But, you know," she said, "I think I did hear it bark."
—BETTY MACK (Wenham, Mass.) May 1958

My hometown in North Dakota was celebrating its 75th anniversary. I eagerly returned for the festivities, positive that I would still know everyone there.

One morning many of us gathered in the old confectionery store, where we hugged one another and began reminiscing. A man walked in. I went up and flung my arms around him. "I can't remember your name," I said, "but I *know* I know you!"

"I doubt that," he replied, hugging me back. "I'm just driving through from California. But this sure is a friendly town!"

—S. W. L. (Phoenix, Ariz.) Oct. 1988

For months, the residents in our small Midwestern town endured the clouds of dirt that swirled about when a main street was torn up for repair. The arrival of the paving crew, therefore, was a major event. Our friend Phyllis was so glad to see them that she dashed into her kitchen and whipped up a dinner of fried chicken and apple pie to feed the work crew. When she presented the pie to the foreman, he said, "Ma'am, if that were a chocolate pie, we'd have paved your driveway too!"

Phyllis laughed. Then she went back into the house and came out with a chocolate pie before heading off to work. When she returned, the crew was gone, and an empty pie plate sat in the middle of a brand-new driveway.

—Frederick J. Chiaventone (Weston, Mo.) Mar. 1995

My husband, Jerry, and I had a neighbor who worked evenings. Without fail, his car's piercing headlights would illuminate our bedroom precisely at 12:20 A.M. as he turned into his driveway. My husband would awaken immediately and deliver a tirade about inconsiderate people.

One night I was roused by Jerry's tossing and turning. "Are you ill?" I whispered.

"No," he said. "But it's nearly 2 A.M., and that guy hasn't come home yet. I'm worried about him."

—Barbara R. Furr (Marion, Ohio) Mar. 1993

I was talking with an old friend on the street one day, when a young man stopped for a few words with us. My friend introduced him, called him son and bragged like a father when the young man left. Knowing that he had no children, I was a bit puzzled.

"Listen," he explained, "as a youngster that neighbor kid pulled my flowers, trampled my hedge and chased my cat. As he grew older, I had to buy magazines and candy for the many causes he was representing. Later, we were startled at odd hours by the roar of his motor scooter or the revved-up engine of his old jalopy. Now that he's turned into a decent chap, I claim part of the credit."

—BECKY HARKINS (Altus, Okla.) June 1968

It was a icy winter night. A friend and I were driving through an unfamiliar neighborhood when our car suddenly slid off the road, landing in a front yard. As we started to shovel, people came out of nearby houses to help. Finally the car was out, and I offered to pay the homeowner for any damages to his yard.

He flatly refused. "It's worth every rut to see adversity bring out the good in people," he said with a smile.

—KEITH MEYER (Ste. Genevieve, Mo.) Feb. 1987

I drove into my company parking lot during a rainstorm and found a good spot only a few steps from the door. Another car approached it from the opposite direction. As I was casting about for a way to resolve this impasse, the other driver smiled and held up a coin. Catching his meaning, I tapped the top of my head.

He tossed the coin, glanced down as he caught it, waved and drove off.

—RICHARD J. CEONZO (Poughkeepsie, N.Y.) Oct. 1987

NATIONAL PASTIMES

SHOPPING SPREE

My father was completely lost in the kitchen and never ate unless someone prepared a meal for him. When Mother was ill, however, he volunteered to go to the supermarket for her. She sent him off with a carefully numbered list of seven items.

Dad returned shortly, very proud of himself, and proceeded to unpack the grocery bags. He had *one* bag of sugar, *two* dozen eggs, *three* hams, *four* boxes of detergent, *five* boxes of crackers, *six* eggplants, and *seven* green peppers.

—BENNYE STEAKLEY (Winchester, Tenn.) Feb. 1984

Standing in front of a boutique, I noticed an impatient-looking young man approach a very attractive woman. "Would you mind talking to me for a few minutes?" he asked her.

"Why?" she countered suspiciously.

"My wife has been in this shop for a long time," the man explained. "But I know she'll come right out if she sees me talking to you."

His wife joined him almost immediately.

—E. C. FORBES, JR. (Luling, La.) Aug. 1989

One day I took my teen-age son shopping for clothes, dragging him into store after store. After a few hours, he complained that his feet were sore, and asked if mine were too. I replied that I let nothing stop me when I was shopping and, to further emphasize my point, added, "I came, I saw, I bought."

"Yeah," quipped my son, recalling his Latin. "*Veni, vidi, VISA!*"

—JUDITH THOMPSON (Destrehan, La.) Apr. 1985

My husband teases me about my devotion to TV's home-shopping channel. I, however, think I'm a wise and thrifty shopper, so I don't consider myself a shopaholic.

One afternoon, as I contemplated the purchase of a gold bracelet, the phone rang. "It's for you," my husband said. "Someone named Robert."

Robert, it turned out, worked for the home-shopping channel and was calling to offer me a subscription to their magazine. Excitedly, I told him how much I loved their products. I admitted to placing several orders in recent weeks, although I had not done so in the last two days because I was embarrassed by my husband's teasing.

"Thank goodness," Robert replied with mock seriousness. "I did notice that you hadn't ordered anything in the last 48 hours, and we were all worried that you may have been ill."

—NANCY MONTGOMERY (Escondido, Calif.) Nov. 1994

One evening after dinner, my five-year-old son Brian noticed that his mother had gone out. In answer to his questions, I told him, "Mommy is at a Tupperware party." This explanation satisfied him for only a moment.

Puzzled, he asked, "What's a Tupperware party, Dad?"

I've always given my son honest answers, so I figured a simple explanation would be the best approach. "Well, Brian," I said, "at a Tupperware party, a bunch of ladies sit around and sell plastic bowls to each other."

Brian nodded, indicating that he understood this curious pastime. Then he burst into laughter.

"Come on, Dad," he said. "What is it really?"

—KENNETH W. HOLMES (Virginia Beach, Va.) Feb. 1995

While shopping in a department store, I accidentally left my purse lying on a counter of handbags. As I turned to retrieve it, a woman picked it up.

"Excuse me," I said politely. "That's my purse."

"Oh no, it isn't," she retorted. "I saw it first."

—TARA LOCKWOOD (Lowell, Mass.) Dec. 1992

As I entered the supermarket, I noticed there were only two shopping carts available and they were jammed together so tightly they looked like one cart. A woman came in behind me and, as I held the handle of one basket, she went to the front of the other and pulled. The carts remained stuck. Then she held on fast while I tried to yank them apart. No luck. As a last resort we both pulled on the carts tug-of-war style.

A woman who had just been through the checkout line came up to us. "You don't need to fight over it," she said. "One of you can have my cart."

—EMMY LOU DAVIS (Clayton, Ohio) Aug. 1990

Searching through row upon row of Christmas trees, my husband Norm and I picked one we liked. Then I noticed the one being held by a woman nearby—the perfect tree. I watched as she carried it around the lot and couldn't believe my eyes when she set it aside.

I ditched ours and ran over to grab the coveted tree. "Aren't we lucky?" I said to Norm. "I do feel a little guilty, however, for taking it before she could change her mind."

"I wouldn't worry," he replied. "She just ran over and snatched ours."

—VICKI SALVESEN (Mission Viejo, Calif.) Dec. 1993

I had been grocery shopping with my friend Alicia, and we were looking for the shortest checkout line. We started at opposite ends, and soon I found one register with a solitary man ahead of me. "Hey, Alicia!" I yelled. "This one looks good."

The customer puffed out his chest and said, "That's the best compliment I've had all day."

—LINDA ERWIN (Remlap, Ala.) Aug. 1993

Our local supermarket had just been equipped with a "talking" cash register. I listened, amused, as a mechanical voice announced each item and its price when the clerk passed it over the scanner. After everything had been checked through, the relentless machine told me the total and, after I paid, the change due.

The cashier, who had not yet spoken, got my change and closed the drawer of the finally silent cash register. Looking at me, she said smugly, "*I* still get to say 'thank you.'"

—CHRISTINE KARGE DEWEY (Evergreen Park, Ill.) June 1988

As we browsed in the gift shop at a popular tourist attraction, my son and daughter, ages eight and ten, asked me to buy nearly everything they saw. Trying my best to discourage them, I kept saying, "But it's all junk." Nevertheless they continued to beg. Finally, I gave them each a $20 bill and told them to buy their own souvenirs.

"Which items do you want?" I asked. Clutching their money tightly, they answered in unison, "It's all junk."

—H. DALE JENNINGS (Mangum, Okla.) Nov. 1994

A friend who had just accepted her first teaching job was spending most of her salary for new clothes. Her father urged her to put the money into a savings account instead. He argued that thrift is a virtue; she insisted that clothes make the woman. When the discussion reached a stalemate, she turned to her brother and asked, "What should I do—put my money into clothes, or put it into a savings account?"

His quick reply: "Put it into whichever draws the most interest."

—KATHRYN FANNING (Syracuse, N.Y.) Mar. 1965

A newly single friend had inherited enough money to stop working. But getting her own credit cards was not easy, since she had relinquished both "acceptable" means of support—a husband and a job. "If only they asked the right questions," she said, frowning over a gasoline-company application form. She filled it out and sent it in.

This application, too, was rejected. Annoyed, my friend wrote back: "I have something much more reliable than a husband or an employer—I have stock in your company. If you're okay, I'm okay."

Her credit card arrived two weeks later.

—K. J. D. (Washington, Conn.) Oct. 1987

A fter an exhausting day at work, I stopped at the supermarket on the way home. Finished, I drove to the grocery pickup spot and honked my horn at the teen-ager lazily leaning against the post. Motioning to my two full carts, I shouted, "I want everything in the back of my station wagon."

He pushed the carts over and began putting my groceries in the car. "You're doing it wrong," I snapped. "I want the bags standing upright."

He did as I asked, and then came up to the driver's window. "I just want you to know that I don't work here, lady," he told me, smiling. "I'm waiting for my grandmother."

—VANNA J. SHIELDS (Sterling, Va.) Sept. 1989

S hopping in a high-tech store, I spotted an item I wanted. After filling out an order form, I handed it to a clerk who tried in vain to enter it on the computer register. Then he disappeared into the back room.

A few minutes later he emerged, shaking his head. "I'm sorry," he said. "There are four of them on the shelf back there, but I can't sell one to you because the computer says we don't have them."

—CATHERINE BELAN MORRIS (Houston, Texas) Dec. 1986

Standing in line at the clothing store's counter, I watched as the woman ahead of me handed the clerk her credit card. The customer waited for a long time while the saleswoman went to verify the account. When she finally returned, the clerk said, "I'm sorry, but this card is in your husband's name, and we can't accept it because the records show he is deceased."

With that, the woman turned to her spouse, who was standing next to her, and asked, "Does this mean I don't have to fix lunch for you today?"

—MARILYN ARNOPOL (Northbrook, Ill.) Feb. 1991

OLDEN GOLDIES

My teen-age daughter wanted to borrow 25 dollars to buy a dress. "I'll pay you back as soon as I get my check," she promised.

"What check?" I asked her.

"Oh," she replied airily, "I'm sending an item to *The Reader's Digest*. It's about the time we went to the Jacksons' and they were having a big fight. On the way home you said you were sure glad you and Daddy never fought over such silly things. And Dad said, oh, yes, you did. And you said, oh, no, you didn't. Then he reminded you about some fights you'd had and . . ."

"Stop!" I ordered.

I didn't lend her the money. I bought her "item" for 25 dollars.

—MRS. LEONARD GUESS (Bisbee, Ariz.) Aug. 1958

Late one evening, I decided to pick up some items at the convenience store. Uncertain that it would still be open, I called. "What time do you close?" I asked the woman who answered.

There was a moment's hesitation. Then she said, "Ten o'clock. But we start giving dirty looks at a quarter of."

—ELENA P. TECHET (Chicago, Ill.) July 1988

"You have been specially selected, Ms. Emery—" the voice on the phone announced.

Before she could continue, I interrupted, "You must have the wrong number."

With just the slightest hesitation, she recovered and informed me, "Well, whoever you are, you have been specially selected to receive an amazing offer."

—STEPHANNI HICKEN (Orem, Utah) June 1995

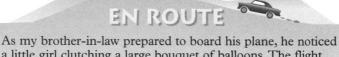

EN ROUTE

As my brother-in-law prepared to board his plane, he noticed a little girl clutching a large bouquet of balloons. The flight attendant reluctantly told her that only one balloon per person could be taken on board. Crying, the child selected her two favorites—one for her father and one for herself—and left the remaining ones behind.

Another passenger had witnessed the incident. Gathering up the balloons, he distributed them to others who were boarding. Destination reached, the happy youngster left the airport, once again clutching her colorful bouquet.

—KAREN K. BAKER (Long Beach, Calif.) Dec. 1985

As the pastor of a small church and the father of a young family, my friend is always looking for ways to cut expenses. One day he was shopping with his wife and noticed that she was about to put an anniversary card for him in the basket with her other purchases.

He approached her to see the card she had selected. After reading it carefully, he looked at his wife and said, "Thank you, dear." Then he quietly returned the card to its place on the shelf.

—T. A. AGNEW (Everett, Wash.) Jan. 1984

After my sister went to college, Dad sent her a credit card to be used for emergency purchases only. "Emergencies," to his distress, soon included new skis and a trip to Las Vegas. Then she came home, and we were at the dinner table. Sniffing the air, Dad said, "Something's burning!" He eyed my sister's purse. "That's it!" Grabbing oven mitts, Dad gingerly removed the much-used card, ran to the freezer and threw it in.

My sister got the point.

—LYNN PAULEY (Charleston, W. Va.) Apr. 1987

In the market for a car, my son-in-law expressed surprise that the new, light makes were practically as expensive as the standard models.

The salesman bristled and replied, "If people want economy cars—they'll have to pay for them!"

—ERNEST OSBORNE (Fire Island Pines, N.Y.) Jan. 1961

In the Eskimo village where I live, the nearest bank is 150 miles away—by dog sled. Because of this, there is a constant shortage of currency. For convenience, signed personal checks are passed back and forth like money.

Once I bought 20 gallons of gas at the village fuel pump and the total came to $61.20. I flipped through my wad of hand-me-down checks and gave the attendant one made out to and signed by a man I'd never heard of. Then I handed her another note from someone whose check would be sure to bounce if it were ever sent to a bank.

As change, the attendant gave me a well-worn check, her last quarter and 32 pennies. "Thanks for paying cash," she said.

—SETH KANTNER (Ambler, Alaska) Jan. 1991

The young man ahead of my father at the flower shop was taking an unusually long time to place his order. When the clerk asked how she could help, he explained that his girlfriend was turning 19 and he couldn't decide whether to give her a dozen roses or 19 roses—one for each year of her life.

The woman put aside her business judgment and advised, "She may be your 19-year-old girlfriend now, but someday she could be your 50-year-old wife."

The young man bought a dozen roses.

—SARAH LYNN ANDERSON (La Mirada, Calif.) July 1991

Shopping in the fine-china department of a store, I noticed a young couple pondering over some patterns. Then a man took the husband aside, and I heard him say, "Son, buy the most expensive china you can afford. Take it from someone who has been married over 40 years, it'll be worth the investment. With china that valuable, you can be assured that your wife will never ask you to wash the dishes when company comes."

—LORETTA J. MICHALCZAK (Hamtramck, Mich.) Feb. 1991

As I waited for my wife outside a lingerie store, I saw a woman entering, dragging her five-year-old son with her. The child, who'd had his fill of shopping, protested, "Mom, do we have to go in here?"

"You said you wanted a little brother, didn't you?" she replied.

—LUTHER E. WALKE (Greenwood, S.C.) Oct. 1993

FROM THE HEART

After shopping all morning, Mother and I stopped at a restaurant for lunch. As we ate, I noticed Mother glancing at a nearby table occupied by an elderly woman and a couple who appeared to be her daughter and son-in-law. They ate silently, and it was clear that things were not going well.

As we rose to leave, Mother stopped by their table. "Excuse me," she said, putting her arm around the unhappy old woman. "It's just that you remind me so much of my mother. May I hug you?"

The woman smiled radiantly as she accepted the embrace, and even turned her wrinkled cheek for my mother's kiss.

After we left the restaurant, I remarked, "That was awfully nice of you, Mother. But I didn't think she looked at all like Gran."

"Neither did I," said Mother cheerfully.

—SARA HUGHES MATHIS (Corinth, Miss.) July 1983

SHAPING UP

Annette, my wife, had bought a membership for me in an exclusive health club. I thought that maybe she, too, would like to join, so I asked her, "Do you want to come with me to the club tonight to see if you would enjoy it?"

"Are you kidding?" she replied. "Not until I lose ten pounds!"

—MIKE GUBOV (Deerfield, Ill.) Feb. 1992

My sister decided to go on a diet, and that first evening she phoned me. I could tell her mouth was full, so I asked her what she was eating.

"A cupcake," she mumbled. "I just got on the scale, and it read 149 1/2 pounds. I decided that was no place to start a diet, so I'm rounding it off to 150."

—SHARON E. ASKEGREEN (Valley Center, Calif.) Nov. 1992

To my surprise, my 40-year-old husband decided to join our daughter Laurel in taking roller-skating lessons. After their first session, Laurel bubbled over with descriptions of "scissors" and "T-stops." "The T-stops are the hardest," she proclaimed.

"And what did *you* find the hardest?" I asked my husband.

"The floor," he moaned, "the floor."

—JOYCE PACHER (Issaquah, Wash.) Apr. 1987

Concerned about his weight, my husband took up jogging. Undaunted by a bitter cold spell, he donned long johns, sweat suit and terry shorts. Next came two shirts, a sweat shirt and a nylon windbreaker. Huge earmuffs under a woolen cap completed the outfit.

"Aren't you afraid you'll look rather silly running in all those clothes?" I asked.

"It's not how I look while I'm *running* that bothers me," he said. "It's how I look while I'm standing still!"

—ELEANOR J. THAYER (Oak Harbor, Wash.) Dec. 1986

A friend of mine had resisted efforts to get him to run with our jogging group until his doctor told him he *had* to exercise. Soon thereafter, he reluctantly joined us for our 5:30 A.M. jogs on Mondays, Wednesdays and Fridays.

After a month of running, we decided that my friend might be hooked, especially when he said he had discovered what "runner's euphoria" was.

"Runner's euphoria," he explained, "is what I feel at 5:30 on Tuesdays, Thursdays and Saturdays."

—NEIL P. BUDGE (Clovis, Calif.) Aug. 1990

F riends of ours, worried about their father's middle-age spread, had been urging him to diet and exercise. The father, however, insisted he was in great shape for his age—until the day his grandson, fresh from observing the various stages of an aunt's pregnancy, approached him as he was watching TV. Patting his grandfather's paunch, the boy asked, "Grandpa, do you have a baby in there?"

"Of course not!" his grandfather hastily retorted.

"Oh!" the child replied. "You mean it's going to *stay* like that?"

There was a new member at the health spa the next day.

—RUTH B. NOÉ (West Chester, Pa.) July 1983

EN ROUTE

As a Pan Am captain, I made the first Boeing 747 landing at Houston Airport. We were taxiing toward the terminal when a DC-9 appeared on a parallel taxiway. It kept up with our speed in order to get a good look at us.

From our cockpit 34 feet above the ground, the DC-9 looked tiny. We were on the same radio frequency, so my copilot hailed them with: "Hello, little brother!"

"Hi!" came the reply from the DC-9. "Wanna drag?"

—KIM SCRIBNER (Garden City, N.Y.) June 1970

A friend wanted me to enroll in an aerobics class. "No way!" I exclaimed. "I tried that once."

"What happened?" she asked, looking puzzled.

"I went, and I twisted, hopped, jumped, stretched and pulled," I replied. "And by the time I got those darn leotards on, the class was over!"

—Louise Osier (Boise, Idaho) Nov. 1988

My diet club meets every Tuesday evening. I hate dieting, so I usually eat as I please all week long and then fast on Tuesday before the dreaded weigh-in. With these eating habits, progress is slow. One day, frustrated by the numbers on my scale, I blurted, "I wish I could lose some of this weight."

"I know how you can do it," my ten-year-old daughter Marvella replied. "Just pretend that every day is Tuesday."

—Jeanne Greene (Santa Monica, Calif.) Jan. 1995

OLDEN GOLDIES

The chairman of our employees' committee had recently given up smoking, and he suggested that we ban cigarettes from all future meetings. His proposal was defeated by a narrow margin.

Later in the meeting, the feminine members were admonished by our somewhat staid office manager to use more discretion in the wearing of mini-skirts. In the silence that followed his remarks, a small voice from the back of the room said, "Guess what he's given up!"

—Sylvan Yates (Santa Ana, Calif.) Apr. 1969

While working out at the gym, I noticed that a middle-aged man on the next machine had stopped exercising. He was sprawled on the lifting bench and slowly turned his head toward his youthful trainer. "When your muscles feel as if they're going to explode," the man asked, "and you think you'll die a slow, painful death, is it time to take a break?"

"Yeah!" exclaimed his young coach. "Isn't it great?"

—MARCO ARTIOLI (Lee, Mass.) Oct. 1993

Astonished, I watched the man roller-skating toward me on the bicycle path. An owl, wings outstretched, clung to a leather patch on his shoulder. As they got closer, I could tell that the giant bird had lost part of one wing. The skater stopped for a breather. "Twice a day we go out so he can pretend he's flying," the man told me.

"I'm sure he would repay you if he could," I replied.

"He already has," the skater said. "I used to weigh 25 pounds more and I smoked." With that, man and bird took off again.

—JAMES EDMINSTER (Chicago, Ill.) Aug. 1988

I had been a heavy smoker since I was a teen-ager, but to my surprise was able to quit "cold turkey." However, my weight shot up, and I felt very self-conscious. When a friend congratulated me on giving up cigarettes, I exclaimed, "But look at all these added pounds!"

Her reply was one I'll always treasure. "Oh, my dear, don't worry about that!" she said. "Just think of all the extra years you will have in which to lose them."

—VERNICE S. SHIRLEY (Greenville, Ala.) Nov. 1986

The pottery-making display at an arts-and-crafts show had drawn a large crowd. I watched as the potter took a big, lumpy piece of clay and worked it until it was a tall, slender vase. When the potter held up the finished piece, the woman next to me sighed and said, "If only they could figure out a way to do that to my hips."

—SANDRA GRIFFETT (Winchester, Ky.) June 1991

SHAPING UP

My tennis partner considers himself a "semi-vegetarian." When he discovered that several of his favorite health-food restaurants gave discounts to members of San Francisco's Vegetarian Society, he decided to join. On the application form, he admitted that he ate fish and poultry "on occasion."

He soon received a cautious reply: "Your membership has been approved. But you cannot vote."

—PETER L. CHRISTENSEN (San Carlos, Calif.) Jan. 1986

My sister Patti was the first of seven children to leave the nest, and Mother was crushed. She worried how her "baby" would manage in a big city without her. After a short time, Patti wrote home. "I've quit smoking, drinking, and I've lost 20 pounds," she bragged.

Mother took a new tack. "Well," she said to the rest of us, "if Patti starts going to church again, the rest of you are moving out too!"

—MELANIE CUMMINGS (Youngstown, Ohio) May 1988

For several months, my family had been excitedly organizing a large reunion in Florida. "Fun-in-the-sun" events were planned, and my sister went on a diet to get ready. When I phoned her, she informed me she had been unable to lose the last ten pounds. "Every ounce of my body knows that I'm going to Florida," she said, "and not one ounce is willing to give up the trip."

—DENNIS CHAPMAN (Virginia Beach, Va.) June 1988

I thought I had finally found a way to convince Susan, my continually harried friend, that she needed to find ways to relax. I invited her to dinner and, while I was busy cooking, she agreed to watch my videotape on stress management and relaxation techniques.

Fifteen minutes later, she came into the kitchen and handed me

the tape. "It was good," she said, "but I don't need it."
"But it's a 70-minute video," I replied. "You couldn't have
watched the whole thing."
"Yes, I did," Susan assured me. "I put it on fast-forward."
—JEAN KELLY (Cumberland, R.I.) July 1990

Caught up in the fitness craze, I joined a club that offered a
reasonably priced membership. Although I never went, a year
later I hurried back to renew. "Do you guys have a name for people
like me who join and never show up?" I jokingly asked the well-
muscled man behind the counter.
"Sure," he responded with a grin. "Profit."
—RANDY PADAWER (Knoxville, Tenn.) Mar. 1989

My daughter couldn't muster the willpower to lose unwanted
pounds. One day, watching a svelte friend walking up our
driveway, she lamented, "Linda's so skinny it makes me sick."
"If it bothers you," I suggested gently, "why don't you do something about it?"
"Good idea, Mom," she replied. Turning to her friend, she called
out, "Hey, Linda, have a piece of chocolate cake."
—DORIS E. FLETCHER (Kendall Park, N.J.) Aug. 1990

My friend and I had joined a weight-loss organization. At one
meeting the instructor held up an apple and a candy bar.
"What are the attributes of this apple," she asked, "and how do
they relate to our diet?" "Low in calories" and "lots of fiber" were
among the answers.
She then detailed what was wrong with eating candy, and concluded, "Apples are not only more healthful but also less expensive.
Do you know I paid thirty-five cents for this candy bar?" We stared
as she held aloft the forbidden treat.
From the back of the room a small voice spoke up: "I'll give you
forty cents for it."
—PAMELA ZMEK (Madison, Wis.) July 1984

When Jackie hit his late 40s, he started jogging. A few weeks later the familiar figure was no longer going past our house. "Have you stopped running?" I asked him.

"The first week I ran one block and walked one block," Jackie began. "The next week I ran two blocks and walked a block. The third week I ran three blocks and walked two blocks.

"The fourth week," Jackie concluded, "the math got so darned hard that I just gave it up."

—CARLA SIMS (Booker, Texas) Aug. 1989

My husband, an exercise enthusiast who spends an hour and a half at an athletic club every morning before work, encouraged a middle-aged—and quite overweight—friend to join him for his morning sessions. The co-worker decided not to tell his wife about his new project until after he had shed the pounds, and he faithfully began meeting my husband at 6 A.M. every day.

At the end of the first week, the friend's wife of many years rolled over in bed and offered this parting advice: "I don't know where you're going, dear, or what you are doing. But just remember: you aren't used to it."

—DEBBI BEAUCHAMP (Baytown, Texas) Oct. 1983

EN ROUTE

It was rush hour in the subway at Grand Central Station and as usual people were trying to force their way into jam-packed cars. I noticed one guard helping to cram them in. After he had pushed one burly man through the door, I complimented him.

"I ain't doin' it for the passengers, lady," he assured me. "I play semi-pro football on Sundays, and this is the only exercise I get to keep in condition."

—MRS. A. GORDON (New York, N.Y.) Jan. 1952

The doctor is constantly urging me to shed extra pounds. At a recent examination, he started in again. "I may have to give up sex and dancing, but I'm not giving up food," I protested.

My doctor was quiet for a moment. Then he asked, "Did you ever think that with a little less food there might be more sex and dancing?"

—MADELINE K. RYAN (Livonia, Mich.) July 1988

Waiting for our aerobics class to begin, several of us were standing around in our leotards chatting about fitness and diets. One woman said that her brother-in-law had quit smoking, gone on a diet and lost weight—all at the same time.

Thinking to myself that no human being could possibly do this without acquiring at least one other undesirable habit for compensation, I jokingly asked her, "What did he start doing instead of these things?"

After a slight pause, she smiled and said, "Well, my sister is pregnant now."

—MARGARET NUTTER (Clawson, Mich.) Jan. 1984

It was apparent from my lunch order at the convenience store— two ounces of chicken and a sugar-free soda—that I was dieting. The owner commented, "I just purchased an audio cassette that guarantees weight loss if you listen to it regularly. It's subliminal. You hear nothing but ocean waves, and it's supposed to change your eating habits."

"How much did you lose?" I asked.

"Thirty-five dollars," he said.

—LINDA S. WENDEL (Middletown, N.Y.) Jan. 1989

To lose weight, I discarded all of the high-calorie, prepared foods in my kitchen and replaced them with dried beans, brown-rice cakes and fresh produce. I didn't realize the effect it had on my family until my son Matt and his friend raided the pantry in search of a snack and came up empty-handed.

Apologizing to his friend, Matt said, "My mom doesn't buy food anymore. She just buys ingredients."

—JEAN M. BORGEN (St. Paul, Minn.) June 1994

SHAPING UP

PLAY BALL!

As a gift, I received a dozen golf balls, each imprinted with my name—Tony Palmigiano. One day, while playing on a public course in Queens, N.Y., I decided to use one of the balls. One of my drives off the tee sliced into the adjacent fairway. As I approached the spot, I saw a woman pick up my ball, look at it and slip it into her golf bag.

When I politely informed her that the ball she had picked up belonged to me, she immediately pulled it out and said, "Oh, no! You see, I always play a Tony Palmigiano ball!" Feeling like a pro, I walked away with a big smile on my face.

—TONY PALMIGIANO (Taylors, S.C.) July 1994

The community softball league couldn't afford to pay umpires, so each team volunteered a member for the thankless task. When my first turn came, I was nervous—ballplayers in our town had been rough on rookie umpires.

"Play ball," I called, in what I hoped was a confident voice. The first pitch came hard and fast. "Strike one," I yelled. The next pitch

was high, and I shouted, "Ball one." I thought this was going to be easy after all.

Then I saw the pitcher walking toward me. "*What* did you call that pitch?" he asked.

"A ball," I said. "It was high."

The pitcher shook his head in disbelief. "Yeah," he replied, "but the batter swung and *missed!*"

—KENNETH L. GIBBLE (Arlington, Va.) Aug. 1990

At a golf course, our foursome approached the 16th tee. The straight fairway runs along a road and bike path fenced off on the left. The first golfer teed off and hooked the ball in that direction. The ball went over the fence and bounced off the bike path onto the road, where it hit the tire of a moving bus and was knocked back on our fairway.

As we all stood in amazement, I asked him, "How in the heck did you do that?"

Without hesitation he said, "You have to know the bus schedule."

—MICHAEL A. LANKFORD (Birmingham, Mich.) Aug. 1995

Our son is an avid sports enthusiast. One day he was in the basement searching for a hockey stick. Suddenly he bounded up the steps holding aloft an old college sweater with an award for excellence in tennis sewn on it. "Dad!" he shouted enthusiastically. "You never told me you earned a letter in college!"

His father slumped a little lower in his easy chair. "No, son, I didn't," he reluctantly admitted. "That tennis letter belongs to your *mother*."

—HELEN MCCLELLAND MYER (Denver, Colo.) Feb. 1987

At my six-year-old daughter's first soccer game, there were lots of excited parents. One woman kept her video camera focused on the field. During a break, I asked her which child was hers.

"I don't have a child on the team," she said. "I'm taping my husband. It's his first time as a referee."

—CONNIE REDWINE (Cincinnati, Ohio) Apr. 1991

My husband, who is in his 70s, returned from playing golf one afternoon and announced that he and his partner had joined up with two attractive young women. "They turned out to be real good golfers too," he added.

"Did you learn anything from them?" I asked.

"I learned that it's impossible to hold my stomach in for two hours!"

—KAY GAMMONS (Cape Elizabeth, Maine) May 1989

Since my wife, a native of Germany, had never been to a baseball game, I took her to see the Los Angeles Dodgers one night. Our seats were right behind the third-base line.

At the top of the first inning, the batter hit a foul ball. Miraculously, I managed to catch it on the fly. As I sat down, breathless with excitement, my wife turned to me and said, "That was nice. How many of those do you get a game?"

—STEPHEN FINNEN (Redondo Beach, Calif.) Apr. 1995

My wife, Diane, was chatting with her brother, Charles, a business executive who had retired last year. While discussing the joys of his new leisure time, Charles remarked that he had been compelled to give up skiing, a sport he had enjoyed for many years.

"Afraid of injuries?" Diane asked.

"Well, now I am," he responded. "Before, I could drag a cast into work and still do my job, but now I'd be messing up my golf game."

—LEO GRANT (Glastonbury, Conn.) July 1992

For several weeks my husband had had trouble getting to sleep at night. I read some articles on relaxation techniques and decided to try one on him. As he got into bed, I said softly, "Imagine that you are sitting on your favorite fishing bank. The sun is warm and a breeze is stirring. Your cork is bobbing up and down, up and down on the water." His eyes closed. Just when I thought I had succeeded, he sat bolt upright in bed.

"But I don't fish with a cork," he said.

—SHERRY A. BRADLEY (Kansas City, Mo.) June 1988

Our parish priest was asked to spend the day on the golf course with two friends. Although he said his game was terrible, he went along anyway.

At the first tee, another golfer joined them to make a foursome.

So as not to make the stranger nervous, the priest insisted they introduce him as "Ron."

On the fourth hole, the other golfer turned to Ron and asked him what he did for a living. Confronted, Ron admitted that he was a Catholic priest. "I knew it!" the stranger exclaimed. "The way you play golf and don't swear, you'd *have* to be a priest."

—JOHN V. R. COPES (Windsor, Conn.) Aug. 1983

On a fishing trip, a friend's canoe tipped over, and he was unceremoniously dumped in icy water. He reached the shore safely and took off his brand-new life jacket to let it dry out. To his dismay, it fell apart.

Later he went back to the store with the pieces of the life jacket and told the clerk what had happened. The man gave him a look of shocked disbelief. "What did you do?" he asked. "Get it *wet?*"

—CINDY BEST (Des Moines, Iowa) Aug. 1989

OLDEN GOLDIES

In this day and age it is often difficult to determine the sex of persons one sees in public places. While on an outing to an ice-skating rink with her eight-year-old daughter, a friend of mine observed a particularly graceful skater whose dress and hair could have been that of either a boy or a girl. When she asked her youngster's opinion, the child replied without hesitation, "It's a boy. He has on black ice skates."

—LAURA HINDERAKER (Idyllwild, Calif.) Dec. 1969

FROM THE HEART

Mose, the rotund and jolly pawnshop owner in my midwest hometown, was always doing nice things for people. One day, as Christmas approached, I saw him busily sorting various articles that had been pawned, gift-wrapping them, and labeling each with a name tag. I asked him what he was up to.

"Well, it's like this," Mose replied. "I figured that these things probably mean a great deal to their owners out at the old folks' home, and I doubt that they will ever be able to redeem them. So, this is my present to those folks this year."

—DOROTHY CALDWELL (Los Angeles, Calif.) Jan. 1967

Jim, my 40-something husband, was playing basketball with friends his age. "Pretty soon," said one of his teammates, "we'll have to count it as a basket if the ball just hits the rim."

"Yeah," Jim agreed. "It's scary when you have to look through the bottom part of your bifocals to shoot layups and the top part on jump shots."

—PAMELA HELMER (Vernon Center, N.Y.) Feb. 1993

Every summer my husband practices his golf swing on our lawn, inevitably breaking a window or two. One year he had trouble with his slice; the number of broken windows rose to four.

The following spring a parcel arrived, addressed to my husband. It was a box of golf balls. The enclosed note read: "Have a good season. From Mike, your window man."

—KAY B. TUCKER (Binghamton, N.Y.) July 1988

At the hockey game, I was rinkside when one of the players rammed into the boards. As he struggled to regain his balance, he gasped, "There must be an easier way to make a living."

"I'll trade jobs," I retorted.

"What do you do?" he queried.

"I teach sixth grade."

"Forget it," he said, and was gone.

—MAURINE K. MUGLESTON (Salt Lake City, Utah) Mar. 1985

My husband, Bruce, usually organizes a foursome to play in the annual member-guest tournament at his golf club. Last year he had two guests lined up and was debating about the third. One of the potential players, a doctor who worked in the emergency room at the hospital, seemed a good choice to me. But Bruce had reservations about him.

"Doc handles life-and-death situations every day," he explained. "He may not understand how important golf is."

—KAREN MACDONALD (Adams, Mass.) May 1992

While raising our first three sons, my wife had put aside her dislike of sports and served as a Little League mother. Now, eight years after the birth of our last son, she was about to have a fourth child.

After the baby arrived, the nurse came out to the hospital waiting room to get me. My wife was on a stretcher being wheeled back to her room when I caught up with her. "Your husband doesn't know what you had," the nurse said, prompting her.

My wife looked up with a drowsy smile and answered, "Another four years of Little League—that's what I had."

—HARRY DEL GRANDE (Greenbrae, Calif.) Jan. 1985

After a shopping expedition, my friend Gina and I stopped in a local bar for a drink. We hadn't been seated long when she leaned over and said that four young men at the next table were watching us. Since we're both "thirty-something," married with children, we found the situation flattering. Naturally we sat a little straighter and tried to look slimmer and younger.

In a few minutes, one of the men got up and came toward our table. "Excuse me," he said. Then he reached over our heads to turn up the volume on the televised ball game that was holding their attention.

—SANDRA LYONS (Cuervo, N.M.) Sept. 1992

After a golf outing, my husband and son David told me how their game had gone. David said his dad had accidentally hit a duck with his golf ball. The bird just quacked and ran off.

"Well," my husband stated defensively, "that duck shouldn't have been on the golf course."

"Dad," David said, "that duck *wasn't* on the golf course."

—SHARON FUGATT (Fort Myers, Fla.) Apr. 1991

EN ROUTE

Last St. Patrick's Day, as my husband was driving to his office, his mind was wrestling with a business problem—and he drove through a red light. Almost immediately he heard at his side the ominous order: "Pull over." But my spouse's inspired words promptly got him off with a wave and a grin. His blue eyes twinkling, his ruddy face aglow, he exclaimed in his best Irish brogue, "Begorra, officer, all lights look green to me today."

—CLAIRE JEAN SPEAKER (Washington, D.C.) Mar. 1958

I live near a lake, and one summer I decided to sell night crawlers. I kept the worms in a cooler on the front porch with a sign that read: "Self-service—put money in container." Customers came and went and, to my surprise, no one took any crawlers without leaving payment.

Once I saw a man with three boys drive up. The kids ran to the porch, took two dozen worms and dropped the money in the container. I approached the man and said how nice it was that there was still so much honesty in the world.

"Ma'am," he replied, "fishermen aren't thieves—just liars!"

—ELSIE R. ST. JOHN (Still River, Mass.) Aug. 1990

Ice-skating on our subdivision's lake one Sunday, my husband, John, and I spotted a large fish lying on the ice. I gingerly picked up the still-living creature and slipped it into the water through a hole cut by an ice fisherman.

Just then two men emerged from a lakefront home. "It's the only one I've caught all day," we heard one shout to the other. "She's a beaut, 23 inches! Come look. I've got her over here on the ice."

—SHEILA K. KLOSTER-PREW (Poplar Grove, Ill.) Feb. 1994

EATING OUT

A t a busy restaurant, my husband and I gave our name to the maître d'. After a while, people who arrived after us were being shown to their tables. "How is it," I demanded, "that we've been kept waiting when we were here first?"

His eyes traveled down his list, and he pointed to our name— which had a line through it. "Madam," he replied coolly, "you've already been seated."

—RHONDA PROSSER (Baltimore, Md.) Jan. 1994

W e spent the first week of our vacation in the Colorado Rockies, traveling in comfortable sport clothes, exploring old mining towns and enjoying the spectacular scenery. When we arrived in Denver on a Friday evening, the bright lights beckoned and we decided to get dressed in our best and go out on the town.

I spent a leisurely hour getting bathed, fixing my hair, applying makeup and selecting the "right" dress, shoes and jewelry. A check in the mirror convinced me that I really should get dressed up more often. It was well worth the trouble.

While my husband finished dressing, I walked over to the motel office and asked the woman manager to suggest a nice spot for dinner and the evening. She looked me over, thought a moment, then said, "Well, do you want to dress up, or just go as you are?"

—JEAN MILLER (Syracuse, Ind.) July 1969

W e were going out for the evening, and I couldn't decide which pair of shoes to wear with my new outfit. I slipped one style of shoe on my right foot, put another style on my left and walked into the living room to get an opinion.

"Honey," I said, "what do you think?"

Glancing up from his newspaper, my beloved replied, "Not that pair."

—CHARLENE LIMONCELLI (San Antonio, Texas) Sept. 1992

O n our honeymoon in New Orleans my husband and I, anxious to sample the famous French cuisine, went to a fashionable restaurant. In our festive mood we ordered the works, including wine and a flaming dessert. When the waiter presented his bill my husband reached for his wallet. To his dismay he found that he had left it in our hotel room. Stammering with embarrassment, he explained the situation to the waiter. Then he hurried off and left me red-faced and flustered. As time passed I began to be terrified that he might not be able to find the wallet and had visions of being compelled to wash mountains of dishes to pay for our dinner. The waiter must have noticed my increasing agitation, for after a few minutes he put me at ease in a manner that epitomized all I had ever heard about Southern chivalry. Coming over to the table, he smiled and said, "That husband of yours sure did leave nice collateral, ma'am."

—GERALDINE RHODES (San Francisco, Calif.) June 1958

Shortly after graduating from college, I joined my kid sister for a Chinese dinner and one of our frequent heart-to-heart talks. She was my confidante whenever I needed advice on women, so our conversations were often intimate.

After one hour of personal discussion, I suddenly became aware of my surroundings. Concerned that we might have been overheard and eager to leave, I quietly asked my sister for the time.

"Nine o'clock," pronounced a woman at the nearest booth.

—Patrick Hocking (Medford, Ore.) Dec. 1994

While driving from New Jersey to Vermont, I took back roads wherever possible. By lunch time I was in a small town and stopped at a restaurant that served homemade soup and pie. As I sat at the counter, a man took the seat next to me. "I'll have a bowl of soup," I told the waitress.

"Make it two," said my unknown companion. We finished the soup in silence, and the waitress asked if I wanted anything more. "Apple pie," I replied.

"Make it two," said my companion, lapsing into silence again.

We finished the pie, and the waitress put the check in front of my companion. At that, the wall of silence broke. Smiling, he turned to me and said, "Want to split it?"

—Edith Hibbert-White (Cambridge, Md.) Feb. 1984

My son and his wife were driving through Missouri and stopped in a small town for a late dinner. The only place open was a supper club, and when they walked in, the hostess told them there was a cover charge.

"But we only want to eat," my son explained. "We didn't come for the entertainment."

"Okay, go ahead," said the hostess. "But if you look like you're having too much fun, we'll have to charge you."

—Auburn Dowdy (Albin, Wyo.) May 1991

My brother came home from college for a visit, and my mother treated him to dinner at an expensive restaurant. Brian has an insatiable appetite, and after he ordered a seafood appetizer, prime rib, salad, dessert and coffee, Mom began to regret her offer.

When the check arrived, she asked my brother if he would be willing to help with the tip. "Sure," he replied. He calculated 15 percent of the tab and handed the bill back to her.

—Susan Dean (Jackson, Miss.) Feb. 1994

My husband and I decided to take our two children, then ages seven and three, to our favorite "adult" restaurant for the first time. The younger child refused to stay in her seat and danced around our table. Her sister, tears rolling down her face, laughed loudly at the three-year-old's antics and pounded the table. Beet-red with embarrassment, my husband warned them through clenched teeth, "If you don't start behaving, you'll never eat out with us again!"

The man at the next table leaned over to his wife. "Look, dear," he said. "Quality time!"

—Deborah Bogorad (Loch Sheldrake, N.Y.) Mar. 1993

On a family vacation in Texas, my brother-in-law Mike exhibited the exuberance of a tourist. At a diner, he and his brothers ordered cheeseburgers. When his meal arrived, the first thing Mike noticed was its size.

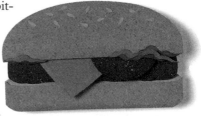

"Wow," he exclaimed, "everything *is* bigger in Texas!"

As he lifted the burger to his lips, his eyes met the cold stare of a 300-pound waitress.

—Kathy Lee (Garland, Texas) Mar. 1995

The diner was filled with young people, but, wonder of wonders, the juke box was singing out only the soft strains of Strauss waltzes. It was such a pleasant change from the usual racket that we couldn't help talking about it. A man sitting nearby overheard us.

"I've got 75 cents in that damned machine," he whispered. "I figure there are enough waltzes lined up to keep off the rack-and-ruin music till we're through lunch."

—SANDRA LEGATZ (Caro, Mich.) Jan. 1960

My husband met me at the doctor's office for my routine checkup, and from there we decided to go out to eat. Since we had driven in separate cars, I arrived at the restaurant first.

"One for dinner?" asked the hostess.

"No," I replied. "There will be two of us in just a minute."

When I saw the panicky look on the hostess's face, I realized I had forgotten about my appearance. Anybody could see that I was at least 8 1/2 months pregnant.

—LOANN K. BURKE (Miamisburg, Ohio) Mar. 1991

Murrells Inlet, S.C., bills itself as the "Seafood Capital of South Carolina." It is home to so many seafood restaurants that it is hard to decide which one to choose.

My wife and I were trying to do just that when we came upon, of all things, a steakhouse. It seemed busy, perhaps because it had adapted to its environment. A sign out front read: "Catch of the Day—COW!"

—CLAUDE G. WHALEY, JR. (Greenville, S.C.) Sept. 1992

A local family restaurant advertises by using the slogan "We've got time for you." Apparently the employees are instructed to use this line when they answer the phone as well. One evening when I was standing in line to pay for an ice-cream cone, the telephone rang. The cashier picked it up and said, "Hello, King's Family Restaurant. We've got time for you. Hold please."

—BRUCE RATHBUN (Monroeville, Pa.) May 1991

We went to breakfast at a restaurant where the special was two eggs, bacon, hash browns and toast for $1.99. "Sounds good," my wife said. "But I don't want the eggs."

"Then I'll have to charge you two dollars and forty-nine cents because you're ordering à la carte," the waitress warned her.

"You mean I'd have to pay for *not* taking the eggs?" my wife asked incredulously. "I'll take the special."

"How do you want your eggs?"

"Raw and in the shell," my wife replied. She took the two eggs home.

—RUSS JENKINS (Hobart, Ind.) Feb. 1985

Deciding to have pizza for dinner, I called one of the pizza houses in the neighborhood and ordered a jumbo deluxe. I told the person on the other end of the line that I'd pick it up in 30 minutes.

When I arrived, my mouth watering for hot pizza, I was told that my order had never been received. Furious, I lectured the young waiter on the poor service before storming out.

On the way home, I stopped at a competing pizza shop and requested a jumbo deluxe. "That's funny," the young man said as he took my order. "You're the second person named Collins to order the same pizza in the last 45 minutes. I don't think the other guy is going to show."

—DAVE COLLINS (Sidney, Ohio) May 1994

SUMMER VACATION

One of the very best parts of our family vacations for me as a child was my mother and her iron. Every year we would get about 75 miles out of town, and she would wail, "Oh, no! I left the iron on." Every year we always turned around and went back. But it was never plugged in.

When I was about 13 years old, we were headed for Yellowstone National Park and, sure enough, almost to the mile marker, Mom gasped, "I just know I left the iron on." My father didn't say a word, just pulled over, got out, opened the trunk and handed her the iron. And every year after that, he made sure that the iron was in the trunk before we left on vacation.

—FRED M. EVERS (Pachuta, Miss.) Apr. 1982

During an overnight fishing trip, we encountered some unseasonably cold weather. We were spending the night on a sandbar, huddled around a fire, hoping to keep warm while we tried to get some sleep. As my nephew stretched out on the sand and pulled his one blanket up around his neck, he remarked with a shiver, "I sure wish I was home in my warm bed, wishing I was up here."

—LYLE DEEM (Parkersburg, W. Va.) July 1969

OLDEN GOLDIES

Recently a teen-age boy was rushed into our hospital with appendicitis. Surgery had been scheduled, so we nurses were puzzled when we heard the boy's mother ask the surgeon if there was a barber in the hospital. "Why do you want to know?" he asked.

"I thought," she replied, "that we might as well get his hair cut while he's under the anaesthetic."

—JAN WINTERS (Angola, N.Y.) Feb. 1968

Suffering through the neighbor's showing of slides from his vacation is a situation familiar to many. But the experience we had while camping in the Black Hills National Forest last summer was quite a switch. No sooner had we pitched our tent than a young man came by to invite us to a neighboring campsite where, with the help of a portable generator, they were showing slides from back home!

—LAWRENCE G. BALCH (Chicago, Ill.) Aug. 1968

Upon learning that I was an Indian national, one of my professors told me about a friend of his who had spent a month touring India. Naturally, he visited the Taj Mahal. Bowled over by the beauty of the building, he and his wife posed for a picture with the Taj serving as an impressive backdrop.

When he returned home, he had the picture enlarged, framed and hung in a prominent space on his living-room wall. Soon after, a good friend stopped by to hear about his trip, marched over to the photograph and exclaimed, "Hey, when were you in Walt Disney World?"

—SANGITA SAMPATH (Toledo, Ohio) July 1994

My husband joined me for a week during my month-long visit to the beautiful Hawaiian island of Kauai. As we walked the beach, I explained that the locals have a casual attitude about time—they never rely on a watch or clock.

Just then, a young man ran up to us and excitedly asked for the time. My husband gave me a smug look as he glanced at his watch and reported the hour. But it was my turn to look smug when the confused young man exclaimed, "No, I mean is it Friday, Saturday or Sunday?"

—KAMALA SILVA (South San Francisco, Calif.) June 1994

SUMMER VACATION

During her vacation, my friend Linda took a guided horseback ride through the countryside. The trail guide, a handsome young man, really looked the part of a western cowpoke. His boots, hat, spurs, even the saddlebags on his horse, appeared totally authentic.

Imagine Linda's dismay when the guide, having lost his way, pulled a cellular phone from his saddlebag and called the ranch for directions.

—JANICE DILL (Newberg, Ore.) Sept. 1992

During our vacation at a dude ranch, my wife told the wrangler that she was an experienced rider. When the spirited steed she'd been given started to bolt, she dropped the reins and hung on for dear life.

As the cowboy caught up to her, he shouted, "Why are you holding on to the saddle with two hands?"

"Because I only *have* two hands!" she yelled back.

—MICHAEL KING (Brooklyn, N.Y.) July 1993

After an exhausting 12-hour drive to our honeymoon destination in Daytona Beach, Fla., my husband and I decided to refresh ourselves with a dip in the motel pool. I must have dropped a few pounds to pre-wedding jitters, because each time I dived into the pool, I lost either the top or bottom of my skimpy new bikini. We had the pool to ourselves, so we just laughed and retrieved the pieces.

Later we dressed for dinner and went down to the motel restaurant. Waiting for a table, we sat in the lounge and ordered drinks. Above the bar was a huge, empty, glistening fish tank.

Curious, my husband asked, "Why is such a beautiful fish tank empty?"

The bartender grinned from ear to ear as he replied, "That's not a fish tank. It's the swimming pool."

—TARA KELLY WALWORTH (Geneva, Ill.) Jan. 1995

While deep-sea fishing in the Gulf of Mexico, I overheard two charter-boat captains talking over the marine-band radio about the difficulties they were having finding fish. Concerned about the 20 passengers who had paid $25 each to catch fish, the apparently less-experienced captain asked the other, "When do we start to panic?"

"Don't panic," the mariner calmly replied. "Just tell them they should've been here yesterday."

—R. MARK WEBB (Fort Myers, Fla.) May 1991

Getting away from their high-stress jobs, friends of mine spend relaxing weekends in their motor home. When they found their peace and quiet disturbed by well-meaning, but unwelcomed, visits from other campers, they devised a plan to assure themselves some privacy.

Now, when they set up camp, they place this sign on the front door of their RV: "Insurance agent. Ask about our term-life package."

—CAROL STURM (Chicago, Ill.) Nov. 1992

OLDEN GOLDIES

The big electronic computer in the accounting department where I work performed admirably until summer weather arrived. Then it practically quit. A diagnosis of the trouble revealed that the machine was extremely sensitive to changes in temperature, so the only thing to do was to move it into an air-conditioned room. Now, as we office drones perspire and droop, we are treated to the vision of the computer operating coolly and efficiently beyond the glass wall of its private office. What was that again about men being smarter than machines?

—Fornia Fill (Los Angeles, Calif.) Aug. 1958

Camping in Yellowstone National Park last year, our friends returned to their campsite and found it invaded by several bears. One large black bear was tossing and slapping an ice chest around like a beach ball, in an attempt to open it for food.

The wife screamed for her husband to go rescue their chest. He watched the bear for a few seconds, then said, "That's not *our* ice chest. That's *his* ice chest."

—E. R. Bailey (Sacramento, Calif.) Mar. 1967

The power Disney exerts over the imagination quickly went to work on us during a visit to EPCOT Center in Florida. Soon we were lost in the illusion that we were actually in France, browsing through the stores and comparing prices.

My companion picked up an item and studied it closely. Turning to me she asked, "Do you think this is cheaper back in the States?"

—Rita Mosley (Denton, Texas) June 1987

We were visiting in Memphis, the former home of Elvis Presley, and I wanted a crossword-puzzle book to work on in our motel room. We were near Graceland, Presley's estate, and the shops featured nothing but Elvis T-shirts, Elvis coffee cups, Elvis books and magazines.

I decided to try one more store. "Do you have anything but Elvis?" I asked the clerk.

"Is that in hardback," she replied, "or paperback?"

—RICHARD J. ENGELHARDT (Nashville, Tenn.) July 1992

After a two-week camping trip, we stopped at the general store for ice-cream cones. "Well, did ya have a good time?" the proprietress asked.

"Great!" I answered. "But how did you know we are ending our vacation instead of starting it?"

"Simple," came the tart reply. "You have a tan, you smell like campfire smoke and your hair looks like hell!"

—JULIA M. SMITH (Coloma, Mich.) July 1987

FROM THE HEART

Although we volunteer firefighters love serving our small town, our lives are often disrupted when our pagers go off. One morning, I was grocery shopping when my beeper sounded, and I rushed out of the store, leaving my shopping cart in an aisle.

When I returned and reclaimed my cart, I discovered it was now full. On top was my grocery list and this note: "I finished your shopping for you. Thanks for helping the community."

—CHRISTOPHER MARTIN (Gaylord, Mich.) Feb. 1994

As I was enjoying the view at an overlook in the Great Smoky Mountains, a family of tourists pulled in. Speaking Chinese excitedly, they started taking snapshots of one another.

I thought they might want a group picture, so I approached one woman. "Excuse me," I began and then, speaking slowly in my Southern accent and using gestures, continued. "Would you [pointing to her] like me [pointing to myself] to take a picture [miming holding a camera] of *all* of you [sweeping my arm to indicate her family]?"

She smiled, handed me her camera and said to the others in perfect English, "This nice hillbilly woman is going to take a picture of us!"

—CHERYL HODGE (Knoxville, Tenn.) Nov. 1993

When we travel, my husband, David, always makes reservations weeks in advance. Our first trip to a small Minnesota town to visit our grandchildren was no exception. David phoned the local motel, and the desk clerk told him the dates we had selected were available. As usual, my husband asked for a confirmation number. "We don't have confirmation numbers," the woman said. He asked for a written confirmation. "I'm afraid we don't do that either," she politely replied.

"After traveling over 700 miles," David demanded, "how will we know that we'll have a room waiting for us?"

"I've written your name in the register in *ink*."

—LINDA PARKS (Muskegon, Mich.) Nov. 1992

EN ROUTE

Flying for the first time, my husband, Mark, and I were both nervous. After a tense but uneventful flight, the plane was still a few hundred yards above the runway as we approached the airport to land. Gazing out the window, Mark heaved a sigh of relief.

"We haven't landed yet," I said.

"I know," he replied. "But I can jump from here."

—RHONDA ADAMOVITS (Ottawa, Ill.) May 1995

Our vacation ended on the hottest day Maine had experienced in years. The station wagon was packed to the roof. One child had to lie down because he was sick, which meant the other three were wedged into the middle seat. I held the baby on my lap.

My husband tied the last suitcase to the top of the car and climbed behind the wheel for the 400-mile drive back to New York. Then he turned around and said, "Just remember one thing. When I yell at you on this trip, I don't mean it!"

—Nardi Reeder Campion (Hanover, N.H.) Sept. 1983

As the long line at a Walt Disney World attraction snaked back and forth, my family and I realized we kept seeing the same people. They began to look like old friends, and we knew it must have seemed that way to them too. When a by-now-familiar woman came into view again, she leaned across the dividing rail and said, "My, how your children have grown!"

—Rosalind C. McCulley (Warrenton, Va.) Dec. 1992

A friend, Elizabeth, fought her fears and joined the trail ride down into the Grand Canyon. As she and her fellow riders descended the narrow track, Elizabeth remained stoic, ignoring the pebbles and small rocks that, loosened by her mule's hoofs, plummeted to the valley floor. But her newfound courage disappeared when she overheard one trail guide remark to the other, while nodding at her mule, "I thought they'd retired old Stumblefoot."

—JOAN M. BRADSHAW (Franklinville, N.J.) Feb. 1991

O n a kayaking trip to the Apostle Islands in northern Wisconsin, my wife and I were talking to our guide as we ate lunch on a remote beach. I mentioned how unusual it was to have no television, newspapers or radio. "In fact," I continued, "it's going to be strange to return home and find out what's been going on in the real world."

No one spoke for a few moments. Then, without taking his eyes from the horizon, the guide replied, "I assumed that's what you came *here* for."

—KEN MCCORMACK (Madison, Wis.) July 1990

OF HOME AND HEARTH

HE SAYS, SHE SAYS

Arriving home from work at my usual hour of 5 P.M., I discovered that it had not been one of my wife's better days. The result was a short fuse and an unpleasant attitude. Nothing I said or did was right. By 7 P.M. things had not changed, so I suggested I go outside, pretend I had just gotten home, and start all over again. My wife agreed.

I went outside, came back in and announced, "Honey, I'm home!"

"And just where have you been?" she replied sharply. "It's *seven* o'clock!"

—DANIEL B. SCHMIDT (Gainesville, Fla.) Oct. 1983

My wife was recently elected president of a women's club in our area. Next morning as we were having breakfast, she wondered aloud whether the job would require too much of her time. From the depths of my superior male knowledge I advised her: "The first thing you have to do is learn to delegate responsibility."

"All right," she said. "Take out the garbage."

—ROBERT E. SCHWEITZ (Fairfax, Va.) Mar. 1968

EN ROUTE

While I was having a cup of coffee at a small café, someone asked the waitress what had happened to the front of her car. She said that her husband had hit a deer, and added, "I'm sure glad he did it. If I'd had the accident, I would have been driving too fast. If our daughter had had it, she would have been driving recklessly. Since he was driving, it was unavoidable."

—SHARON GREENFIELD (Fossil, Ore.) Jan. 1968

Recently engaged, I asked my Aunt Jane, who has been married to Uncle Bob for 34 years, what she thought was the key to the success of their long union. She began, "We try not to argue, and we respect each other's privacy—"

At this point Uncle Bob interrupted. "She works days and I work nights," he said.

—DAN SMOLLA (De Kalb, Ill.) Jan. 1988

One afternoon, during a drive in the country, a squabble broke out between a friend of mine and her husband regarding his driving habits. Finally in frustration she proclaimed, "I'm the only woman alive who would put up with you."

"I'll have you know," he said, "that hundreds of women went out with me in my bachelor days."

His wife replied straight-faced, "I can understand the large turnover."

—DEBORAH SNYDER (Buford, Ga.) Sept. 1983

Lonn and I were involved in a petty argument, both of us unwilling to admit we might be in error. "I'll admit I'm wrong," I told my husband in a conciliatory attempt, "if you'll admit I'm right."

He agreed and, like a gentleman, insisted I go first. "I'm wrong," I said.

With a twinkle in his eye, he responded, "You're right!"

—JEANNINE BUCKLEY (Centerville, Utah) Mar. 1993

With a group of local women, I was helping to prepare a benefit luncheon. My daughter was soon to be married, and we were all relating personal stories about marital situations and how we had managed them.

One of the women, a native Alaskan who is married to a Dane, said, "When Karl and I have an argument, I yell at him in Eskimo and he yells at me in Danish. That way we do not hurt each other's feelings."

—MRS. DONALD JUDD (Spenard, Alaska) May 1968

My parents had not been out together in quite some time. One Saturday, as Mom was finishing the dinner dishes, my father stepped up behind her. "Would you like to go out, girl?" he asked. Not even turning around, my mother quickly replied, "Oh, yes, I'd love to!"

They had a wonderful evening, and it wasn't until the end of it that Dad confessed. His question had actually been directed to the family dog, lying near Mom's feet on the kitchen floor.

—MARY M. TRIVIGNO (Livingston, N.J.) Dec. 1987

OLDEN GOLDIES

My friend Gordon, a student from England in the United States on a university fellowship, nearly got run down in San Francisco by a gentleman driving a Cadillac. Although my British friend was at fault, the driver stopped and apologized and, on top of that, invited Gordon to have lunch with him at his club. Gordon was delighted, but he was puzzled by the man's actions when they got to the club. The Cadillac man steered him directly into the writing room, sat him down at a desk and saw that he had pen and paper.

"Now, my boy," he demanded, "how long has it been since you wrote your parents?"

"Well, I've only had time to send them a couple of post-cards," Gordon said apologetically.

"I'll be back in half an hour to take you to lunch," his host told him. "In the meantime, you write them a nice long letter—it's my cover charge to all the foreign students I've brought here."

The letter Gordon's parents received a few days later was the best they had had.

—Iris Shear (London, England) Feb. 1956

My husband, Mike, and I had several stressful months of financial difficulties. So one evening I was touched to see him gazing at the diamond wedding ring that symbolized our marriage.

"With this ring…" I began romantically.

"We could pay off Visa," he responded.

—DAWN HILL (Houston, Texas) Feb. 1994

When a co-worker announced one morning that he and his wife were expecting their first child, we all gathered around to congratulate him. Someone asked whether he wanted a boy or a girl, and he replied that he didn't care what it was—all he wanted was a healthy baby.

So I asked, "What about your wife? Does she have a preference?"

"Oh," he replied, "she wants a boy too!"

—CONSTANCE MURDOCK (Philadelphia, Pa.) Aug. 1994

Before the arrival of our son, my husband and I attended birthing classes at the hospital. One day we toured the maternity ward. The instructor mentioned that on the last evening of our stay we'd be given a complimentary dinner for two, and she told us what the menu selections would be. As we continued the tour, I whispered to my husband,

"Honey, I'm getting so excited."

"Me too," he replied. "I'm going to order the lobster."

—KATIE SCHNEIDER (Grand Rapids, Mich.) Aug. 1991

I was attending a community-education course on effective parenting. Ways of dealing with children's behavior were discussed. At the last class, the instructor asked a very frazzled-looking mother of two, "Have any of these methods helped you handle your kids better?"

"No," the woman responded. "But they've worked wonders with my husband!"

—LYNN G. KEINATH (Ortonville, Mich.) Sept. 1987

It's hard to win an argument with my wife. The other day she was expounding to the man next door her ideas on women's rights. "Certainly there are physical differences between men and women," she admitted. "But in temperament, intellect, and in all other ways, there is no difference!"

"How do you know that?" he pressed.

"Women's intuition," she replied.

—WILLIAM COWLING (Seattle, Wash.) Aug. 1969

My buddy Glenn invited me to lunch to meet his fiancée, Jennifer. As a surprise, I asked Becky, a mutual friend, to join us. At the last minute, Glenn called to say that Jennifer had some work to do, so they might be delayed. I told him that Becky was planning to meet us and it was too late to reach her with a time change.

"Would your fiancée let you go to lunch with two women she doesn't know?" I teased.

"Are you kidding?" Glenn responded. "I'm a man of the '90s."

"Does that mean you can come?"

"No," Glenn replied, "that means I have to ask."

—BEVERLY A. BRICE (Hagerstown, Md.) Mar. 1993

I was attending an outdoor music concert with a young man I'd recently begun dating. Standing at the back of the crowd, we wrapped our arms around each other, swaying to the music. After a particularly romantic song, my date turned to face me. With a loving smile he said, "I wish we were closer..."

Totally thrilled, I looked into his eyes and whispered, "Do you mean our houses or our friendship?"

Puzzled, he replied, "...to the stage."

—MISSY PICKETT (Reno, Nev.) May 1994

Prior to our wedding, David and I met with the minister to discuss our marriage ceremony and various traditions, such as lighting the unity candle from two individual candles. Couples usually blow out the two candles as a sign of becoming one. Our minister said that many people were now leaving their individual candles lit to signify independence and personal freedom.

He asked if we wanted to extinguish our candles or leave them burning. After thinking about it, David replied, "How about if we leave mine lit and blow out hers?"

—CARA SUE TAUCHER (Burgettstown, Pa.) Apr. 1991

EN ROUTE

When our 18-year-old daughter told us she was going to drive alone from North Carolina to upstate New York, my husband and I suffered qualms of parental concern. But when she arrived—safe and sound—she told us a story that brought tears to our eyes.

On the route north, she kept passing and being passed by several big trucks. She drove her little car between the trucks on level spots, and then passed them when they slowed down on hills. Grins and waves were exchanged as the miles rolled by. Near Baltimore, the trucks tooted a farewell and took a road heading east.

When our daughter stopped for gas in Pennsylvania, a trucker came up to her. "Are you 'Little Sister'?" he asked.

"Pardon me?" she said, surprised.

"Is that your little car with the New York plates?" he persisted.

She answered yes, and he said, "Glad to see you're okay. Truckers down Carolina way have been on their CBs telling everyone to watch out for 'Little Sister' 'cause she's traveling alone."

—P. M. (Schenectady, N.Y.) Mar. 1984

We were visiting friends when they received a telephone call from their recently married daughter. After several tense minutes on the phone, the mother told the father to pick up the extension. The newlyweds had had their first big fight.

In a few moments, the father rejoined us and tersely explained, "Said she wanted to come home."

"What did you tell her?" I asked.

"Told her she *was* home."

—LARRY CUNNINGHAM (Billings, Mont.) Aug. 1993

After directory assistance gave me my boyfriend's new telephone number, I dialed him—and got a woman. "Is Mike there?" I asked.

"He's in the shower," she responded.

"Please tell him his girlfriend phoned," I said and hung up.

When he didn't return the call, I dialed again. This time a man answered. "This is Mike," he said.

"You're not my boyfriend!" I exclaimed.

"I know," he replied. "That's what I've been trying to tell my wife for the past half-hour."

—LAURA MILLER (Bowling Green, Ky.) Jan. 1993

When a new permanent turned out to be a disaster, I phoned my husband and issued a one-line warning: "Don't say anything about my hair."

During dinner, we discussed the weather, his day at the office—anything but my hair. I began to feel uneasy. Finally, when we were washing the dishes, he said in a serious tone, "You'd better go now. My wife will be here any moment, and she wouldn't like finding me with a strange woman."

—J. KAY PATTERSON (Baton Rouge, La.) Apr. 1985

One evening my husband's golfing buddy drove his secretary home after she had imbibed a little too much at an office reception. Although this was an innocent gesture, he decided not to mention it to his wife, who tended to get jealous easily.

Later that night my husband's friend and his wife were driving to a restaurant. Suddenly he looked down and spotted a high-heel shoe half hidden under the passenger seat. Not wanting to be conspicuous, he waited until his wife was looking out her window before he scooped up the shoe and tossed it out of the car. With a sigh of relief, he pulled into the restaurant parking lot. That's when he noticed his wife squirming around in her seat. "Honey," she asked, "have you seen my other shoe?"

—JOAN FELDMAN (Southfield, Mich.) Feb. 1992

My husband's uncle thought he had conquered the problem of trying to remember his wife's birthday and their anniversary. He opened an account with a florist, provided him with the dates and instructions to send flowers along with an appropriate note signed, "Your loving husband."

His wife was thrilled by this new display of attention and all went well until one day, many bouquets later, when he came home, kissed his wife and said offhandedly, "Nice flowers, honey. Where'd you get them?"

—CELIE THOMAS (Mechanicsville, Va.)
Mar. 1993

One day my sister was enjoying a favorite snack when her husband remarked, "You're getting a little broad across the beam." She promptly went on a diet. A few weeks and many lost pounds later, my brother-in-law commented, "You should stop losing weight. Your face is beginning to look wrinkled."

"George," came the frustrated reply, "you had better make up your mind which part of me you enjoy viewing more, heads or tails."

—MARGARET M. HAYNES (Boise, Idaho) May 1984

One day I commented to my wife about her recent weight gain. She began to protest, but I reminded her that our relationship was based on honesty.

"Our relationship is not based on honesty," she retorted, "It's based on flattery, and it's rapidly going downhill."

—STEPHEN M. McMILLION (Summersville, W.Va.) May 1993

I was glancing over the cover of a women's magazine I'd just bought. One title caught my eye: "Men's Secret Fear About Their Working Wives." I decided to get a firsthand account. "What's your innermost fear about my working?" I asked my husband.

"That you'll quit," he promptly replied.

—LINDA G. McCLENON (Plantation, Fla.) Mar. 1987

A couple I know were discussing their wallpaper, which had just been hung. Dov was annoyed at Debby's indifference to what he felt was a poor job. "The problem is that I'm a perfectionist and you're not," he finally said to her.

"Exactly!" she replied. "That's why you married me and I married you!"

—B. N. M. (Chicago, Ill.) May 1988

R ecently married, my wife and I were doing errands and discussing current events. Soon we got into an argument over the issues.

I reiterated my position forcefully, but Christine had the last word. "When I knew I'd found Mr. Right," she snapped, "I had no idea his first name was Always!"

—PAUL KESSLER (Brooklyn, N.Y.) Feb. 1994

FROM THE HEART

Our daughter Becky wrote to her husband every day after he was deployed to the Persian Gulf last August. In addition, she frequently sent him "care" packages to make desert life a bit more tolerable.

Since Becky couldn't get to the post office during the week, I often mailed packages for her. Once, while checking a parcel's customs tag, I noticed that my daughter had itemized each object and its value. The last thing listed was: "All my love. Value—priceless."

—Carolyn Walker (Jacksonville, Ark.) May 1991

My husband's grandparents, married for more than 50 years, went to a restaurant for lunch, where Papa ordered a Reuben sandwich.

"He'll have the red snapper," Gram brusquely told the waitress. "He doesn't *like* Reubens."

"I'll have the Reuben," Papa shot back.

"Red snapper!"

Papa sighed in resignation. Shrugging, he explained to the waitress, "When you've been married as long as I have, you get set in *her* ways."

—RENEE THOMPSON (Lacey, Wash.) Sept. 1985

My husband retired, and for the first time in 40 years I had to think about preparing a midday meal. Tired of it after several months, I said, "I married you for better or worse, but not for lunch."

"Fair enough. From now on I'll make my own," he replied.

A few weeks later he had to go downtown on business and invited me to join him afterward. "We could have lunch at that Japanese restaurant we both like," he suggested. I happily agreed.

At the restaurant the next day we were seated, and the waiter came to take our order. My husband looked up, a twinkle in his eyes. "Separate checks, please," he said.

—SYLVIA BARON (Albuquerque, N.M.) Jan. 1989

EN ROUTE

On a business trip, I was stopped by a state trooper for speeding on a Massachusetts interstate. Thinking it might help my cause, I said, "Officer, for the past 30 years I've driven an average of 40,000 miles per year, and this is my very first speeding offense."

The trooper wrote the ticket, handed it to me and said with a smile, "We should have caught you a long time ago."

—JOE DERVIN (Framingham, Mass.) Aug. 1995

Although many men in our rural area have difficulty accepting women's lib, my husband helps with the housework. One day he took over the vacuuming while I went to the store. The doorbell rang. It was one of his friends—a burly ranch foreman clad in a battered cowboy hat, faded jeans and worn boots. "I was just cleaning," my husband said somewhat abashed, turning off the vacuum. The rancher looked relieved. "That's all right," he said gruffly, handing my husband a white paper bag. "*I'm* delivering Avon!"

—C. ELAINE CRAWFORD (Oleta, Okla.) Feb. 1987

A friend of mine is one of today's working mothers. After coming home from teaching school, she juggles her remaining time among three young sons, household chores and extracurricular activities. One day, after participating in a 4-H project, we walked wearily into her house. As she passed her husband, she gave him a hug and said, "I really love you."

He grinned and asked, "How much?"

"Let me count the ways," she said, dropping into a chair. "The way you washed that tubful of dirty jeans. The way you ran the dishwasher. The way you picked up the boys from the baby-sitter's. But especially the way you stand by me instead of just sitting down."

—ANDREA MCCLUSKEY (Billings, Okla.) July 1984

On a visit to Chickamauga and Chattanooga National Military Park in Georgia, I stood at Wilder Tower. On this site my great-great-grandfather Burkhart, a Union officer, had helped defend Army headquarters from a Confederate attack in which my great-great-grandfather Simpson had taken part.

A young couple was standing nearby, and the wife asked me, "Did you have a relative who fought here?"

"Yes," I replied. "My great-great-grandfathers on my mother's side exchanged shots on this very spot."

As they walked away, I heard her say, "You see, honey, every family has in-law troubles."

—MIKE PATTY (Maryville, Tenn.) May 1993

POTLUCK

My cooking has always been the target of family jokes. One evening, as I prepared dinner a bit too quickly, the kitchen filled with smoke and the smoke detector went off. Although both of my children had received fire-safety training at school, they did not respond to the alarm. Annoyed, I stormed through the house in search of them.

I found them in the bathroom, washing their hands. Over the loud buzzing of the smoke alarm, I asked them to identify the sound.

"It's the smoke detector," they replied in unison.

"Do you know what that sound means?" I demanded.

"Sure," my oldest replied. "Dinner's ready."

—DEBI CHRISTENSEN (Mission, Texas) Aug. 1995

When we were first married I didn't know how to cook and flopped badly in my attempt at lasagna. Fifteen years later, I tried again. My husband came to the table and glanced at the food.

"What!" he exclaimed. "Lasagna again?"

—IRENE MUNIZ (Brandon, Fla.) Oct. 1987

Shortly after our 23-year-old daughter, the "Microwave Princess," moved into an apartment, she came to our house for dinner. As we were doing the dishes, she asked if she could take the leftovers home. Pleased that she had enjoyed the meal, I packed the food in microwaveable containers.

She had been gone an hour when I heard footsteps running up to our front door. I opened it, and there she stood with a sly grin. She had invited a young man over for a home-cooked dinner the next day, and she needed to borrow some pots and pans for "special effects."

—BOBBIE S. CREECH (Wilson, N.C.) Jan. 1991

We had invited our friends Bob and Sheila to a special dinner. While my wife, Lee, prepared the meal, I rushed out to buy just the right wine.

Everything seemed perfect as we sat down at the dinner table, until I noticed that the ice bucket held an inferior wine. "Honey," I said, "please bring out the bottle I purchased tonight. Bob and Sheila deserve better than this."

"Dear," Lee replied quietly, "Bob brought the wine."

—DON URQUHART (Valencia, Calif.) Feb. 1994

While lodging a couple of nights at a small New England farm, I was asked if I liked porridge. I admitted my weakness for it, but was embarrassed next morning when I was the only person to be served a huge plate of the steaming cereal. I gently admonished the farmer's wife for going to so much trouble on my behalf. "Oh, that ain't no trouble at all," she assured me cheerfully. "Had to make it for the pig, anyway."

—MRS. P. A. JONES (Oxford, Nova Scotia) Feb. 1967

OLDEN GOLDIES

Every year the many nationality groups of Cleveland join in an all-nations exhibition and food fair. Browsing there last year, I noticed that the booth operated by the women of British descent was not doing a particularly brisk business. Their fine imported biscuits were being bypassed in favor of more exotic offerings.

When I passed the booth later that afternoon, business had greatly increased. The new customers were mainly teenagers. A closer examination showed why. The fare was unchanged, but in the center of their display the enterprising matrons had placed a large photograph of a familiar foursome, with a sign proclaiming: "Genuine Beatle Food Sold Here."

—LINDA FLECK (Cleveland Heights, Ohio) Apr. 1965

After a few months of marriage, I took my city-bred bride home to meet my family. It was her first taste of farm life, and she was also a bit nervous about meeting all her in-laws at once. Wanting a chance to show her domestic skills, she offered to help prepare the big Sunday dinner. "Can you clean chickens?" asked my somewhat skeptical mother.

"Oh, yes," replied my bride brightly. "That's easy—you just pull out the little plastic bag!"

—W. DAVIDSON (Pico Rivera, Calif.) Apr. 1969

Expecting my new in-laws for dinner in a few hours, I still had no idea what to cook for these dear but finicky gourmets. I called my mom for some menu ideas, and she suggested beef stroganoff. She dictated the recipe over the phone and then, as an afterthought, told me to be sure to add some wine.

"To the beef, as it's simmering, or to the noodles?"

"To *you*," she instructed, "just before your guests arrive."

—SARAH E. HALL (Storrs, Conn.) July 1983

One afternoon my younger sister, Connie, phoned me. "I have company coming for dinner tomorrow," she said, "but I can't decide what to serve."

I gave her some simple recipes for a complete menu. Surprised that she hadn't contacted our older sister, who is an excellent cook, I asked Connie, "Why didn't you call Loydaine?"

"Because," she replied, "I knew that if *you* could make it, I could."

—DEBBIE GRONNING (Casper, Wyo.) Feb. 1993

It was shortly before dinnertime, and I had to drive my son's friend home first. After quickly pounding and breading boneless chicken breasts and layering them with marinara sauce and Parmesan cheese, I put the foil-covered pan into the oven. Then I set the timer so they would bake while I was in the car.

As I was leaving, my husband arrived from work. "I'll be back soon," I said. "If the timer goes off, would you please take the foil off the pan, sprinkle the chicken with mozzarella cheese and put it back in the oven for five more minutes?"

Rolling his eyes, he replied, "I really don't feel like cooking tonight. Can't you just stop and pick up a take-home meal?"

—WENDY L. KAUFMAN (West Redding, Conn.) Dec. 1994

When our company expanded, I began to work longer hours and didn't realize the effect this had on my home life. After several days of takeout food served on paper plates, I finally found the time to fix a home-cooked meal. When we finished eating, my daughter said how nice it was to have "real food for a change" and then promptly threw her china dish in the trash.

—GLENDA MONACO (Grandview, Mo.) July 1991

For our first New Year's together as a married couple, my wife offered me a choice of pumpkin pie, cheesecake or orange-date cake. "Pumpkin pie," I requested.

"We've been eating pumpkin pie ever since Thanksgiving," Nancy protested. "Can't you choose something else?"

"Okay," I replied, "how about cheesecake?"

Making a face, Nancy said, "After all that rich food you ate over Christmas, surely you don't want cheesecake."

Recognizing my limited options, I then selected orange-date cake.

"Orange-date cake is a New Year's tradition in our family," Nancy informed me. "I'm so glad you chose that one."

—PETER HARDWICK (Watertown, N.Y.) Jan. 1992

While on vacation in Florida, my wife and I made plans to visit her grandmother. On the morning of our visit, we called to let her know we'd show up around dinnertime.

When we arrived at five o'clock, Grandmother was annoyed. "Where have you been all afternoon?" she asked. "I had a nice big dinner ready for you at one o'clock!"

Confused, I replied, "At one o'clock? You mean lunch?"

"That's dinner!" she snapped.

"Dinner is supper," I argued.

"No, supper is supper," she countered. "Dinner is lunch."

"Well, if you put it that way, we had dinner before we left," I said. "So what's for supper?"

Throwing her hands up in the air, she said, "Dinner."

—CHRIS LUNDQUIST (Richland, Wash.) Oct. 1994

My busy mother would sometimes accidentally leave pots and pans on the stove with the burners on, so she resorted to posting this reminder on the kitchen door: "STOVE?"

When my sister returned from college, she noticed Mother's sign. Beneath it she taped her reply: "No—door. Trust me. I went to college."

—KIRSTIN OSWALT (Winchester, Ind.) July 1993

Telephoning my daughter one afternoon, I first got her husband on the line. "What are you doing?" I asked.

"Oh, just cooking some spaghetti and making a salad," he replied.

I told him what a prize he was to help out around the house, and then asked to speak with my daughter. "Can she call you back?" he said. "I hate to interrupt her." He paused. "She's . . . uh . . . mowing the lawn."

—P. A. G. HOEHLE (Columbia, Mo.) July 1983

Our church was planning a chili supper for the homeless, and my wife, Florence, agreed to prepare four gallons of her rather mild variation. The man in charge of organizing the program asked Florence how she would describe her chili—three alarm or four alarm. After hearing some of the ingredients that went into other chili donations, my wife replied, "I guess you'd call mine false alarm."

—J. C. BJORKHOLM (Richmond, Va.) July 1991

EN ROUTE

My brother John and his wife, Ann, embarked on an eight-hour train trip to Buffalo, N.Y. They met their train in Whitehall, N.Y., near the Vermont border. It was behind schedule, so they were an hour late departing. A setback in Schenectady resulted in another hour-and-a-half delay. As they pulled out of the Schenectady station, the train stopped again.

Apparently, a train traveling ahead of them on the same track had hit and injured a cow. Neither train could proceed until the cow was removed from the tracks. The engineer of John's train recalled passing a rail switch about four miles back, so he decided to back up to the switch and then continue to Buffalo on the parallel track.

After a long, slow backup, they were on their way again. But as they pulled up beside the first train, the cow struggled up from the tracks, staggered and fell—directly in front of my brother's train.

—PATRICIA A. MEYER (Elyria, Ohio) Apr. 1995

THE FAMILY CAR

The day Tim, the youngest of my three children, got his driver's license, he invited the three of us to go with him. I was determined not to spoil the day with advice or words of caution.

Tim must have picked the narrowest, most winding, hilly road in the area. Unfazed, he and his brother and sister discussed automobiles and how to repair them. As we flew along, I kept a smile on my face and my mouth shut.

When we came into the home stretch at the driveway, I sighed and congratulated myself for my forbearance. Just then my daughter asked, "Tim, what kind of tool would you use to remove Mom's fingernails from the upholstery?"

—JOAN QUINN (High Bridge, N.J.) July 1993

Our teen-age daughter, Cathy, had just been given family-car privileges. One Friday night she returned home from a party late. The next morning her father went out to the driveway to get the newspaper and came back into the house frowning.

At 11:30 Cathy sleepily walked into the kitchen to face the question "What time did you get in last night?"

"Not too late, Dad."

"Then I'll have to talk with the paperboy about putting my paper under the front tire of the car" was her father's straight-faced comment.

—SUSAN SCHUSTER (Grosse Pointe, Mich.) July 1989

When my aunt backed the family van into the garage, she accidentally knocked off a side mirror. "Someone hit the van while I was shopping at the mall," she told my uncle upon his return from the office. "The culprit didn't even leave a note. Can you imagine the nerve?"

"The guy had more nerve than you think," my uncle replied. "He even followed you and put the broken glass in our garage."

—LYNN SOWERS (Hubbard, Ohio) Feb. 1994

Grandfather is known for always driving well below the speed limit. One Sunday my grandparents were going to attend a family gathering. "Hurry or we'll be late!" Gram repeatedly urged him. He continued on just as slowly. Finally Gram could take it no longer. "Stop the car, dear, and let me out," she said in her sweetest voice. "I'll run on ahead and tell them we're coming."

—MICHELLE JOHNSON (Ontario, Ore.) Feb. 1988

When a friend asked my husband what kind of gas mileage he was getting on his new sports car, he answered, "Well, as nearly as I can figure, *I* get about four miles to the gallon and my teen-age son gets the other 11."

—MRS. R. L. WILLIAMS (Kettering, Ohio) Jan. 1968

When a tornado hit our shopping mall, my friend Greg and I were worried about his parents, who owned a store in the complex. We hopped into my banged up, rusty 1971 Pinto and made our way there.

It looked like a war zone. Cars were torn apart, and news crews and firemen were running about. After checking on Greg's parents, we left the chaotic scene. That night, on a TV newscast about the tornado, the announcer said, "And here is a sample of some of the damage done to vehicles in the parking lot." The camera moved in for a close-up of my Pinto.

—DAN JACKSON (Becker, Minn.) Sept. 1994

My Aunt Goldie is known for her love of activity. Anyone who invites her out usually gets an enthusiastic "Yes!" in response.

One day her husband, John, went outside and got in the car. "Wait!" Goldie yelled as she rounded up the kids. She quickly ran a brush through her daughter's hair and changed her son's shirt. Then, grabbing her purse, she raced through the door. As her husband waited wordlessly, she buckled the kids in the back seat and collapsed in the front. "Okay," she beamed at him. "Let's go."

John took the car out of park and drove into the garage.

—CAROL HOLDERBY (Oklahoma City, Okla.) Feb. 1995

When I was in high school, musical car horns were popular. My mother's deluxe model played the first line of 48 different songs. But when it was extremely cold, the horn sometimes developed a short and played on its own. I urged Mom to take it out of our car, but she refused to get rid of it.

That is, until the cold winter afternoon that Mom and Dad attended a graveside funeral service for an elderly aunt. As they were pulling out of the cemetery, the horn blared the first stanza of "We're in the Money." I never heard the horn again.

—ROSIDA PORTER (South Solon, Ohio) Mar. 1994

Chad, my friend's son, was at that awkward age—old enough for his first date, but too young to drive. He gave his chauffeur/father strict instructions: "Just drive. Don't turn around, don't try to talk to the girl and don't embarrass me!"

My friend took Chad to pick up his date and stared straight ahead as his son opened the car door. When he heard it slam shut, he followed Chad's wishes and drove away in silence. As they went down the street, the date shyly leaned forward and said, "Excuse me, sir—Chad didn't have time to get in the car. He's still standing in my driveway."

—SHERRY DONALD (Clarksdale, Miss.) May 1991

After the last of their four children left for college, our friends changed their life-style. They sold their house, bought a condominium and took up new activities. Everything went smoothly until one of their daughters came home, planning to use the family car. When she found that Mom and Dad were going out and needed it, she voiced her complaints bitterly.

"Yes, dear," my friend soothingly said to her daughter. "It's really rough when your parents grow up and move away from home."
—JUDY RIESLAND (Hemet, Calif.) Mar. 1985

As a modern mom who spends much of her time chauffeuring her children to various activities, I sometimes feel as though my life is spent in a car. At the end of one exhausting day, after I had put my kids to bed, I flopped into an armchair in the living room. Automatically my right hand reached over my left shoulder—to fasten the seat belt.
—BONNIE HEATHERLY (Vinemont, Ala.) Dec. 1992

OLDEN GOLDIES

Two lads, parked in a Model T Ford on the edge of Highway 66, signaled me to push them. Assuming that they were out of gas, I eased in behind them and started the old car rolling. After 30 miles we reached a filling station, but the car did not turn in. I got out and asked why they didn't stop for gas.

"What for?" one of them said. He raised the hood of the Model T—and, of course, there was no engine.
—LOUISE MILLSAP (Idabel, Okla.) Jan.1950

COUCH POTATOES

A few days before New Year's, some of my friends and I were discussing how we intended to celebrate. Dances and parties were mentioned most often.

Then one guy, a true reflection of the electronic age, said, "I think I'll turn on the TV and watch the ball drop at Times Square. On second thought, maybe I'll tape it and watch it in the morning."

—MARY LOU ASCHERL (Hinckley, Ohio) Jan. 1993

My fellow construction workers were discussing the TV programs they had watched the previous evening. One man mentioned his remote-control device, which he used to change channels from his easy chair.

"That is one luxury I can get along without," said another man. "It's a sad day when I get so lazy that I can't tell my wife or daughter to get up and change the channel."

—E. J. REGYNSKI (Baldwin Park, Calif.) Aug. 1983

EN ROUTE

A friend of mine was enjoying his new car's powerful sound system by driving along with the volume way up. At a traffic light, he heard someone shout, "Hey, do you mind?"

Stopped next to him was a young man in an open convertible. He pointed to an object in his left hand and said, "Can't you see I'm on the phone?"

—DENNIS DIGGES (Oak Harbor, Wash.) May 1992

My mother and I returned to my parents' house late one evening to find my father, my college-age brother, Steven, and my ten-year-old sister fast asleep. Mom had forgotten her house keys, so we knocked loudly, first at the back door and then the front and side doors. We yelled my father's name over and over, with no answer. The car horn aroused the neighbors but no one at our house.

We drove into town and phoned home, waking Steven. When we got back, he let us in. Dad was in bed, snoring, with the television on. Mom quietly switched it off.

Dad woke right up. "Don't turn that off," he said. "I'm watching it!"
—CHRISTINE WINTERS (Mason, Mich.) Nov. 1992

Our family was having a lively discussion in front of the fireplace when a friend of mine stopped by unexpectedly. "It's so gratifying to see a family spending quality time together," she said. "I wish mine could do the same."

Embarrassed by the truth, I simply smiled and nodded. We had just been arguing about who had lost the TV remote control.
—FRANCES MAIER (Southampton, Pa.) Oct. 1993

I was enjoying the second week of a two-week vacation the same way I had enjoyed the first week: by doing as little as possible. I ignored my wife's not-so-subtle hints about completing certain jobs around the house, but I didn't realize how much this bothered her until the clothes dryer refused to work, the iron shorted and the sewing machine motor burned out in the middle of a seam. The final straw came when she plugged in the vacuum cleaner and nothing happened. She looked so stricken that I had to offer some consolation.

"That's okay, honey," I said. "You still have me."

She looked up at me with tears in her eyes. "Yes," she wailed, "but *you* don't work either!"
—J. L. FREDERICK (Kingston, Ill.) July 1983

Television offerings were scant, and my husband finally settled on a PBS nature broadcast. As we watched, two male crickets waged a fierce battle to win the favors of a female. The victorious male then mated with his prize.

"That's television," my husband said, sighing. "Wherever you look, nothing but sex and violence!"

—REBA D. DUNCAN (Tallulah, La.) April 1987

The lecturer addressing a group of parents was expounding on the evils of television and its contribution to juvenile delinquency. "You turn on your set and what happens?" he challenged. "The worst kind of violence and crime, the most unspeakable degeneracy, brutality . . ."

At this point, a man in the audience remarked in a stage whisper, "And that's only the news!"

—EILEEN GOODMAN, Oct. 1965

One of my co-workers told us he and his wife were going to start a fitness program. That weekend they planned to buy an exercise bike.

A few days later, I asked how they liked the new machine. He said, "It was too big for my wife—and I didn't like the way it was made. We traded it in for a VCR."

—RICHARD A. SAGER (Quicksburg, Va.) June 1993

The dental hygienist was having difficulty removing nicotine stains from my teeth. I'd been trying to overcome my addiction to cigarettes so I asked her if she smoked. "Oh, yes," she replied. "Both my husband and I are trying to quit. We only allow ourselves to smoke outside the house."

"What a great idea," I said. "Is it working?"

"Yes," she replied wistfully. "But we're getting tired of watching TV through the patio doors."

—DOLORES GRUNDISH (Houston, Texas) Aug. 1992

OF HOME AND HEARTH

When my husband came home from work and found the house a complete wreck, he exclaimed, "What happened!"

"You're always wondering what I do all day," I said. "Well, here it is—I didn't do it."

—MRS. LOWELL T. MORGAN (Hillsboro, Ohio) Nov. 1965

Determined to have one last, lazy day of fishing before summer's end, I purposely ignored the leaky faucet and the broken gate—household projects that had awaited me all summer. When my wife asked, "What are you going to do today?" I grinned and answered, "It starts with F and ends with ISH."

"Oh, good," she replied. "You're finally going to FinISH up those projects."

—MIKE MAYBERRY (Manchester, Mo.) Aug. 1994

I had gone to a lumberyard to buy two posts for my new hammock. "How long will the posts last once they are sunk in the ground?" I asked the clerk.

"Longer than you will," he responded. Encouraged, I bought them.

Another customer who was standing nearby grinned and asked, "Did it ever occur to you that he might be saying that you're not looking all that well?"

—LEO GRANT (Glastonbury, Conn.) May 1988

It was a warm fall morning, and my husband decided to come home from work early to paint our deck. Before I left the house, I located all the necessary supplies and wrote him a note: "I put the paint in the closet downstairs. The brush is on the garage shelf."

When I returned that evening, nothing had been done. My husband had left this written explanation: "I found the paint and the brush. Couldn't find the deck. Went fishing."

—CAROL SPONAUGLE (Scott Depot, W. Va.)
Oct. 1987

Last fall, after a stressful workday followed by a two-hour freeway commute, I looked forward to relaxing and watching the next game of the World Series. I was also eager to see what progress the contractor had made in replacing our old wood roof.

When I got home, I nearly went into shock. My yard was covered with beer cans and shingles, and mounds of wood blocked the front door. Furious, I called the roofer on my car phone and yelled at him about my miserable workday, the traffic, the beer cans and the game I was missing.

Unruffled, he calmly announced, "There is no game tonight."

"That figures, considering how my day has gone," I barked. "Was it rained out?"

"Not exactly," he replied. "When I was trimming the overhang today, I accidentally cut your television cable."

—DON CULVER (Orange, Calif.) Nov. 1994

When my friend got a job, her husband agreed to share the housework. He was stunned by the amount of effort involved in keeping a house clean with small boys to pick up after, and insisted that he and his wife shop for a new vacuum cleaner.

The salesman gave them a demonstration of the latest model. "It comes equipped with all the newest features," he assured them.

The husband was not convinced. "Don't you have a *riding* one?" he asked grimly.

—PAT MONTGOMERY (Harborcreek, Pa.) May 1987

OLDEN GOLDIES

A couple we have known for years bought a television set, one of the first in their neighborhood. The husband, a gregarious fellow, told his friends to drop in to see TV whenever there was a program of interest. As a result, during baseball season, Julie, his wife, soon had a stream of callers in the afternoon.

One day as I was driving past their house I noticed a large sign, television today, on the front porch. Curious, I stopped in. "You aren't bragging, are you, Julie?" I asked.

"Indeed I'm not," she replied. "But I found out the neighbors were gossiping because I have so many men in here while Ed is at work. The blinds down, too! This is the best way I can think of to let them know I'm still an honorable woman!"

—VIRGINIA L. HAMILTON (Pittsburgh, Pa.) June 1950

FAMILY TIES

As a single parent with a teen-age son, I have gone through many financial difficulties. Consequently, we live in an old mobile home with all sorts of structural problems. When one of my son's friends, who lives in a beautiful house, ran away for a few days, I was puzzled. "Why did he do it?" I asked. "He has everything he could possibly wish for."

"Well, Mom, it's like this," my son said matter-of-factly. "Jimmy has a lot of environment, but not much love, and I have a lot of love but not much environment."

—CAROL LEINEN (Pearland, Texas) Dec. 1985

Pregnant with my first child, I watched with excitement as my obstetrician did an ultrasound. He gave me a photograph of the baby, who at twelve and a half weeks resembled an extraterrestrial.

When my husband and I showed the picture to my mother-in-law, she looked at it skeptically. "Hmm," she said, turning to me. "The baby must take after your side of the family."

—SHERRY HUNTER (American Fork, Utah) Feb. 1993

FROM THE HEART

During high school, my friend Sue was dating her steady boyfriend. Each night as he backed out of her parents' driveway, she'd flip the front-porch light on and off. When her father asked the reason, she explained that it was her way of saying "I love you."

A year after graduating, Sue decided to move into an apartment. As she pulled out of the driveway with the last of her belongings, her father stood wistfully by the front door and switched the porch light on and off.

—MARCY J. LAWRENCE (Richfield, Minn.) Oct. 1993

I come from a large, close-knit family that has lived in the same rural area of Maryland for 200 years. My husband, an only child with few relatives, found it difficult to sort out all my uncles, aunts and cousins. At one gathering, I remarked, "Maybe I should make a family tree to help you."

"Family tree?" he asked. "Don't you mean family *forest?*"

—EMILY JANE WILLIAMS PERRY (Herndon, Va.) Feb. 1989

I ran short of money while visiting my brother, and borrowed $50 from him. After my return home, I wrote him a short letter every few weeks, enclosing a five-dollar check in each one. He called me up and told me how much he enjoyed the letters, regardless of the money; I had never written regularly before.

Finally I sent off a letter and the last five-dollar check. In my mail box the next week I found an envelope from my brother. Inside was another $50.

—SUZANNE ATTEBERY (Portland, Ore.) Feb. 1984

I was holding my 18-month-old grandson, telling him that he was the sweetest, most adorable precious lamb in the world. Glancing up, I saw my burly, rough-looking neighbor leaning against his motorcycle, looking amused. Embarrassed, I remarked, "You probably never heard such carrying on in your life."

"Sure I have," he said, grinning. "Every time I visit my mom."

—M. E. GARAND (Long Beach, Calif.) Sept. 1988

The family was viewing old slides and one flashed on the screen that caught everyone's attention. My father, wearing his favorite golf shirt, was holding me at the tender age of three weeks. The look on his face told all.

"There's my prize possession," my father said. Touched, I smiled at him as he continued, "I wonder whatever happened to that golf shirt?"

—JEANNE GRAVES (Mobile, Ala.) Apr. 1989

While I was recuperating from surgery, my mother and mother-in-law both offered to help with my very active two-year-old. My mother came first. Five exhausting days later, she got in the car with my husband to drive to the airport where *his* mother was now due to arrive. "Where are you going?" a neighbor's child asked.

In a tired voice, Mother answered, "He's taking a used grandma to the airport and picking up a fresh one."

—JANET O'DAY (El Paso, Texas) May 1986

One morning, my parents offered to watch my two children while I ran errands. Before I could leave their house, my two-month-old began to cry. For over an hour, as my parents tried to help me with my inconsolable baby, my two-year-old followed us about, badgering us with requests to read or play.

By the time the baby settled down, my exhausted parents were more than ready for all of us to go. As I packed up the children's things, I remembered that I had not gone to the bank, so I asked my dad to lend me some cash.

As we got into the car, I heard my irritated father say to my mother, "I had to pay them $25 to leave."

"Don't worry," she quickly replied. "It was worth every penny."

—MARY L. THOMPSON (El Paso, Texas) May 1995

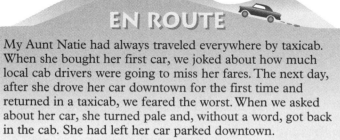

EN ROUTE

My Aunt Natie had always traveled everywhere by taxicab. When she bought her first car, we joked about how much local cab drivers were going to miss her fares. The next day, after she drove her car downtown for the first time and returned in a taxicab, we feared the worst. When we asked about her car, she turned pale and, without a word, got back in the cab. She had left her car parked downtown.

—BIENVENIDO RODRIGUEZ (Rock Island, Ill.) July 1995

An octogenarian in our town was known for her lively sense of humor. Since she lived on the same street as her son and his family, mail mix-ups often occurred.

One day one of her grandsons, home from college, received a letter from his girlfriend. To his chagrin, the envelope had been opened, and then taped shut again. Across the front his irrepressible grandmother had scrawled: "Delivered incorrectly. Opened accidentally. Enjoyed thoroughly!"

—MARY S. RICHARDSON (Marion, Mass.) Nov. 1987

My husband's 96-year-old grandmother came to live with us after many years of ornery independence. We did everything we could to make her transition to our home comfortable, including giving her a private phone line for her bedroom.

One evening when we were entertaining guests, the phone rang. It was a telephone operator, who asked, "Do you have a grandmother upstairs?"

"Yes," my husband replied.

"Well," the operator continued, "she can't remember your phone number, and she would like a cup of tea."

—JUDY RENIUS (Huntington Beach, Calif.) Aug. 1991

My wife and I were invited to her niece's wedding breakfast. During the meal, the groom's father asked all of the grandparents to offer words of advice for a long and happy marriage. It was a poignant moment as each one shared such wisdom as "Never go to bed angry" and "Treat each other as you would like to be treated."

When they finished, the groom's father asked the young couple if they had any words of advice for the rest of us.

"Well," said the groom, to the embarrassment of his bride, "the only thing I can think of is 'Call before you come over.'"

—JAMES E. BLACK (Centerville, Utah) Apr. 1995

My 16-year-old brother, Ryan, was out late with friends one night. Suddenly he realized it was Father's Day and he had neglected to buy a card for our dad. After much searching, Ryan located an open store, but was disappointed to find only two cards left on a picked-over rack. Selecting one, he brought it home and, somewhat sheepishly, presented it to our father.

Upon opening it, Dad read this message: "You've been like a father to me."

He looked at Ryan, puzzled.

"Well, Dad," Ryan tried to explain, "it was either that or the card that said, 'Now that I'm a father too...'"

—ANNE CARLSON (Bay City, Mich.) June 1995

OLDEN GOLDIES

A hippie couple—beads, long hair, sandals, and all—came to the large hospital where my cousin is employed. The woman was taken directly to a room, while her companion was escorted to the admissions clerk to supply pertinent data required. When the question of religious affiliation came up, the young man hesitated. "Well," said the clerk, "is she a Protestant?"

"Uh," stammered the hippie, "not exactly. I don't really know."

"Perhaps I should put down 'None' for the time being," suggested the clerk.

"Oh, no," protested the man. "I'm sure she was never one of those!"

—KEN SIEGEL (Hemet, Calif.) Mar. 1969

Recently my sister, who lives several hundred miles away, called to see how I was doing. When I related some unhappy family news, she said, "You seem to be taking it well."

"Oh," I replied, "I've felt so much better since I smashed a plate into a hundred pieces."

A few days later, I received a package from her. It contained a letter of support, a check to use for phone calls, and an array of old, ugly plates.

—DEBORAH KING (Dover, N.H.) Oct. 1994

We kept in touch by telephone with our son Tim, who had married and moved to Tennessee. However, after several expensive phone bills, I sent him a letter explaining that I would start writing more often in order to save money. Three days later I received a collect call from Tim.

"Hi, Mom," he said. "I just called to tell you I got your letter."

—CHERYL D. BRANDT (Vineland, N.J.) Jan. 1995

My husband's book on Indian treaties and laws had just been published. Since he considered it heavy reading for nonhistorians, he was surprised to hear his mother say she had gone through the entire text. "When I gave you a copy, I didn't expect you to do that," he protested.

"Son," she answered, "if your mother doesn't read it, who will?"

—CAROLYN HOSEN (Lakewood, Colo.) Feb. 1988

My sister, Sharon, and I are close, and that allows us to be honest with each other. As I fidgeted in front of the mirror one evening before a date, I remarked, "I'm fat."

"No, you're not," she scolded.

"My hair is awful."

"It's lovely."

"I've never looked worse," I whined.

"Yes, you have," she replied.

—PATRICIA L. SOUZA (Newport, Ore.) Apr. 1993

When my husband was transferred, I found myself 350 miles from familiar turf. His cousin, who lived in the area, tried to get me used to my new surroundings, but with little success.

A last-ditch effort was made one spring morning. A delivery boy showed up with a potted tree, a gift from the cousin. This note was enclosed: "Once you plant this, you'll have roots here."

—VAL BENNETT (Butler, Pa.) Apr. 1986

It was a large wedding, and afterward the photographer took a long time getting family groups together for pictures. The groom sat by me, waiting with barely concealed impatience. "Now I'd like to get the bride alone," the photographer finally announced.

Leaning toward me, the groom whispered, "So would I!"

—EDITH M. WHIPKEY (Cameron, W. Va.) Apr. 1989

Our nephew had married a beautiful Hawaiian woman he met when they were attending a school on the mainland. A year later they flew to Hawaii to introduce Tom to Geri's family.

In the islands, it is customary for relatives to line up at the airport arrival gate and greet family members with leis and kisses. Tom responded with enthusiasm. Later, nearly smothered in leis, he sought out Geri in the crowd. "That was some reception," he exclaimed. "The women got more beautiful and kissier as I went down the line. But what happened to you?"

"Nothing," Geri said, giggling. "I quit when we reached the last of my relatives. You worked your way through another entire family!"

—JAMES F. COOPER (Tucson, Ariz.) Mar. 1984

On the way to our wedding reception, I said tenderly to my brand-new husband, "It's really special the way your mom and dad love each other so much after all their years of marriage. The thing I think is especially thoughtful is that each morning he brings a cup of steaming-hot coffee to her in bed. Is that an inherited quality?"

"You bet it is!" my husband said. "I take after my mother."

—MARY PARKINSON (Lawrence, Kan.) Sept. 1988

A large inlaid map of the world is set in the floor of the airport terminal where my daughter works. One evening she came upon a young couple sitting on the map having dinner. It was evident that they had tried to make the setting elegant with a linen tablecloth and goblets.

My daughter, who is responsible for the traffic flow in the building, asked them what they were doing. When she heard their explanation she didn't have the heart to ask them to move. They had just been married, they said, and this was the closest they could come to their dream honeymoon.

They were sitting exactly over Hawaii.

—C. B. N. (Walla Walla, Wash.) July 1984

EN ROUTE

My wife's uncle, a Kansas farmer, drove an old pickup that had seen better days. Once, as he and my brother-in-law were rattling along, a loud noise suddenly came from the rear of the truck. "What was that?" my brother-in-law asked.

Uncle just looked straight ahead and replied, "Don't know. Couldn't have been too bad—we're still going."

—AL MANETH (Scottsdale, Ariz.) Jan. 1991

When I was pregnant, we lived in a small town 15 miles from the nearest hospital. Since my husband spent a lot of time traveling in a company car, his co-workers agreed to notify him by two-way radio if I was taken to the hospital.

The great day arrived. Excited colleagues called my husband, who immediately sped to the hospital and dashed to the maternity floor. "My wife is having a baby!" he breathlessly announced to the nurse.

The nurse consulted her records. "She hasn't come in yet," she said.

"Well!" my nervous husband exclaimed. "I just thought that *one* of us should be here."

—PAT LAMAR (Irving, Texas) Dec. 1984

EN ROUTE

Dennis and I almost missed our honeymoon flight and were unable to get seats together. When we were airborne, I wrote my new spouse a flirtatious note: "To the man sitting in 16C. I find you very attractive. Would you care to join me for an unforgettable evening? The lady in 4C." A flight attendant delivered it.

A few minutes later she returned with a cocktail. The man in 16C was flattered, she told me, but said he must decline my offer since he was on his honeymoon. I was still laughing when we landed. "Thank you for the drink," I said to my groom.

"But I didn't send you one," he replied.

He had been sitting in 14C.

—CINDY J. BRAUN (Kennesaw, Ga.) Oct. 1988

On a visit home from college, I found my father listening to one of the many records in his beloved collection. "Dad," I announced, "I have a surprise for you. I'm getting married."

He congratulated me and held out a record. "Son," he said, "remember that marriage is like one of these. You get what you like on one side and take what you get on the other."

—RONNIE JOHNSON (Swainsboro, Ga.) Apr. 1993

Our 22-year-old son, the last of our five children to leave home, was about to move into his own apartment. I had decided to redecorate his room, and asked him to please get all his things out of it.

Roger took the news in an apparently blasé manner. Then, as he left the house, he betrayed his real feelings with this poignant farewell: "I'll be back next week to pack up my childhood."

—ALLAIRE B. NOWNES (Hampton, N.H.) Oct. 1985

While I was browsing in the dress section of a department store, another shopper struck up a conversation with me. "My daughter is getting married soon," she told me, eyes glowing. "She's engaged to a *doctor.*"

After the woman left for the dressing room, the bride-to-be approached and apologized for her mother's interruption. "Oh, it was no bother," I replied. "She told me how happy she was that your fiancé is a doctor."

"Yes," she said with a sigh. "But Mother always neglects to tell people that I'm a doctor also."

—KIM MCDONALD (Mt. Vernon, N.Y.) May 1993

Matt and his bride were opening their wedding gifts. After unwrapping each package Lisa would exclaim enthusiastically, "We can really use these towels" or "We'll enjoy eating on these pretty dishes." Then she opened one very large box. It contained a vacuum cleaner.

"Matt," Lisa said, "look what *you* got."

—LORRAINE SAUNDERS (Mesa, Ariz.) Dec. 1987

A friend's daughter was getting married, and the days just before the wedding were hectic. One night I helped prepare a large dinner for out-of-town guests. After the dishes had been cleared away, the happy but exhausted mother of the bride joined everyone in the living room. As she sat down, she softly said, "When this is all over I plan to stay in bed for a week."

A big smile came over the face of her future son-in-law. "So do I, Mrs. B! So do I!" he boomed.

—MARY ANN MILKO (Lake Orion, Mich.) Feb. 1984

In our local department store, a salesperson was waiting on a young woman whose recent wedding we had both attended. The new bride asked to see twin-bed sheets. The clerk bit her lip as she rummaged through the packages on the shelf. Finally she burst out, "It's none of my business, but *twin* beds? You're practically still on your honeymoon!"

It was the saleswoman's turn to blush as the bride picked out one package of sheets. "You're taking it for granted that we have *two* twin beds," she replied.

—PATRICK CLEPPER (Arden Hills, Minn.) May 1984

After the blizzard, my husband's mother phoned and I lamented that we were almost snowed in. "Whatever you do," she cautioned, "don't send Jack out to shovel snow. It's too dangerous. The radio reports that several people have dropped dead of heart attacks."

"I'll probably end up doing the shoveling myself," I sighed.

"Well," she cautioned, "don't forget to bundle up good."

—A. T. FINN (Dayton, Ohio) Mar. 1968

My mother-in-law and I were discussing a promotion we hoped my husband, Jerry, would get. "He's one of the best people they have," she said. "He works hard, is dependable and doesn't get sick."

"That's right," I agreed. "During the two years we've been married, he has been ill only twice."

"And Jerry was *never* sick before that!" my mother-in-law added.

—LISA GWEN ROARK (Rio Rancho, N.M.) Dec. 1992

EN ROUTE

While flying from Denver to Kansas City, Kan., my mother was sitting across the aisle from a woman and her eight-year-old son. Mom couldn't help laughing as they neared their destination and she heard the mother say to the boy, "Now remember—run to Dad first, then the dog."

—KARLA J. KASPER (Ankeny, Iowa) Feb. 1991

GENERATIONS

When I took my baby daughter to the supermarket for the first time, I dressed her in pink from head to toe. At the store, I placed her in the shopping cart, put my purchases around her, and headed for the checkout line.

A small boy and his mother were ahead of me. The child was crying and begging for some special treat. *He wants some candy or gum and his mother won't let him have any,* I thought.

Then I heard his mother's reply. "No!" she said, looking in my direction. "You may *not* have a baby sister today. That lady got the last one!"

—MARSHA PRIESMEYER (Garwood, Texas) Sept. 1985

Early in her third pregnancy, my neighbor took her two active pre-schoolers to the bank with her while she conducted some rather lengthy business. The bank teller gave them jellybeans from a candy dish and began working. All was quiet for a while, but then the children grew rambunctious. As their mother struggled to maintain order, she heard the teller say cheerfully, "Have another one."

Too harried to notice the candy dish in his hand, she wailed, "That's just the trouble! I'm going to!"

—DIANE S. BRUCKERT (Maynard, Mass.) May 1984

EN ROUTE

I was driving my father and grandfather down a rough country road. My inexperience in handling Grandpa's four-wheel-drive vehicle made for a particularly bouncy ride. Embarrassed, I offered a lame excuse, "The sun shadows through the trees make it hard for me to see all the potholes."

"Don't worry, Matt," Grandpa said. "You're gettin' most of 'em."

—MATTHEW WALKER (Brandon, Vt.) Aug. 1992

The birth of our second child, a daughter, came after a long and difficult labor. But it was definitely worth it when our beautiful little girl emerged, perfect in every way.

Later, in my room, my husband looked at her tenderly, with tears in his eyes. Then as he glanced up at me, I expected him to utter something truly poetic.

Instead he asked, "What's her name again?"

—CHRISTINA L. MILLER (Greencastle, Pa.) Jan. 1995

The day our first child was born, my husband was ecstatic—and his concern for me was truly tender. Five years later, after the birth of our fourth son, he was somewhat more casual. He walked into my hospital room after work and, seeing me for the first time since delivery, he slumped into the chair next to my bed and exclaimed, "Whew! What a day *I've* had!"

—LOIS SOCKOL (Newton Center, Mass.) July 1968

When my oldest daughter received her kindergarten registration form, I was surprised and a little apprehensive about answering all the personality and social-development questions. Meeting a neighbor whose son was also registering, I asked her what she thought of the questionnaire. Her answer summed up my feelings completely. "I'm torn," she said, "between telling the truth or giving him a good start."

—RUTH DINKEL (Hamburg, Pa.) Oct. 1968

When my husband and I went to the local preschool to pick up our four-year-old son, Tony, we asked the teacher about his behavior. Smiling, she commented on how bright and attentive he was. Proud that his behavior reflected positively on our home life, we watched as Tony and a group of boys and girls played in the miniature kitchen area nearby.

Suddenly, Tony stepped up to the toy refrigerator, flung open the door and exclaimed at the top of his lungs, "Hey! Anybody want a beer?"

—TAMMI SALAMUN (Palo Cedro, Calif.) May 1995

My daughter Lois told me that some boys as well as girls had been visiting my 13-year-old granddaughter. Assuming that I'd gained some wisdom from years of child-raising, I warned my daughter against too much freedom in the early mingling of the sexes.

"Mother," Lois replied with certainty, "if the boys weren't here, the girls would meet them on the corner." I reminded her that boys never came to our home when she was only 13.

It was time for me to learn the truth. "I told them not to," Lois confessed. "I met them on the corner."

—JENNIE LUNDQUIST (Bridgeview, Ill.) Sept. 1992

We leave home early in the morning, so my wife and I trust our teen-age daughters to get themselves dressed and off to school on time. One Saturday, I ran into a woman who asked if I would be getting my daughter Ellen an alarm clock for her birthday. Puzzled, I asked her why she thought Ellen needed one.

"Because I'm her homeroom teacher," she answered.

Later that morning, I found Ellen in our kitchen, still in pajamas, eating her breakfast.

"Guess who I just talked to?" I asked.

"Who?" Ellen responded.

"Mrs. Morales," I replied.

Without missing a spoonful, Ellen looked up at me and said, "Who's she?"

—MEL MOYER (Griffin, Ga.) Apr. 1995

My sister and I were comparing our own adolescence with that of today's generation. I commented that there were no demonstrations or protest groups in our day, and instead of expensive and faddish new clothes we wore hand-me-downs. "But," I concluded, "we didn't complain."

"No," replied my sister thoughtfully. "We didn't know we could."

—Mrs. A. W. Eversfield, Oct. 1968

Pat was going to school full-time, working part-time, and raising a family. When she asked one of the kids to help by hanging up a coat or making a bed, the usual response was, "I'm going to use it later."

One day Pat had had enough. After dinner she opened a kitchen cabinet and piled the dirty dishes in it. "What are you doing?" a shocked child asked.

"We're going to use them later. Why bother to wash them?" Pat answered.

The kids started hanging up their coats and making their beds.

—Carol Boissonneault (Taylor, Mich.) May 1988

On my way to Seattle, I stopped to phone my wife, only to discover that she was in the hospital having our first baby. I headed back. As I finally neared home, I was driving fast. A voice came over the CB: "What's your hurry, buddy?"

"We just had a baby," I said, struggling to keep my voice even. "I don't even know what it is."

As I rounded the crest of the next hill, I could hardly believe my eyes. Trucks and cars had all moved into the right-hand lane. The word had gone out and, to smiles and waves, I was given an open road the rest of my way home to meet my new son.

—David Dixon (Cedar Rapids, Iowa) Aug. 1984

When summer arrived, my teen-age son became increasingly irresponsible about the chores he was supposed to be doing around the house. He wouldn't even help to train our new puppy. As a single, working parent, I felt overwhelmed.

Finally I went to the library to get a book on dog training. As an afterthought, I also picked up a book called *Teenagers: The Continuing Challenge*, and took both to the checkout counter.

The librarian glanced at my selections. "The dog is going to be a lot easier," she commented dryly.

—L. T. J. (Washington, Pa.) Aug. 1985

My teen-age son was at that rebellious stage when a parent's endorsement of anything is the kiss of death. So I was pleased he asked me to help him pick a shirt to wear to a party. On his bed were the choices: blue, white and beige. "I like the blue one," I said.

"What's your second choice?"

"The white one."

"Thanks," he said—and put on the beige shirt.

—SYBIL CALLAHAN (Royal Oak, Mich.) Nov. 1988

My friend Jim was a typical first-time father. Not long after his son was born, he ran into an acquaintance in a restaurant and, over coffee, filled him in on all the statistics. "He's 21 days old today," he concluded.

"Why, that's very nice," replied the patient listener.

"Nice?" said Jim. "For a three-week-old boy, that's darn good!"

—HERMAN WREDE (Gardena, Calif.) Dec. 1968

My stepson, the father of two preschoolers, often spells out words he doesn't want his sons to add to their vocabularies. After one grueling day, my stepson was exhausted. Turning to his wife, he said, "We really shouldn't say 'damn' in front of the k-i-d-s."

—JOYCE EVERETT (Hampton Bays, N.Y.) Apr. 1987

I came home from work one day to find my wife, JoLynn, cradling our six-month-old daughter and repeating, "Da-da, Da-da." How sweet, I thought to myself, for her to choose *Daddy* as our baby's first word.

Several weeks later, JoLynn and I were wakened by a small voice crying, "Da-da."

Turning over to go back to sleep, my wife said, "She's calling you, dear."

—MIKE COLEMAN (Manchester, Mo.) June 1993

As a new father, I quickly learned the true meaning of maternal instinct. Late one night, I was summoned to the hospital to attend to one of my patients. I quietly got up in the dark but tripped over a toy and crashed to the floor. As I lay there rubbing my sore leg, my wife slept on.

Then there was a faint cough from the nursery. Debra leapt out of bed, running past me down the hall to our baby's room. When she returned, she looked at me and said, "What on earth are you doing on the floor?"

—ROBERT C. MURRAY, JR., M.D. (Brentwood, Tenn.) Aug. 1993

My wife and I were in a restaurant watching the antics of a young child at the table across the aisle. She was running around, alternately wheedling and pouting, and laughing at her harried mother's attempts to keep her in her seat. Finally the little girl came to a stop at our table, clutching the edge with grimy hands and staring at each of us before charging off again.

My wife, herself a veteran of three children, sighed. "I don't know her name," she commented, "but her phase is familiar!"

—JAMES A. WARNE (Sanborn, N.Y.) Apr. 1986

GENERATIONS

When my three-year-old son opened the birthday gift from his grandmother, he discovered a water pistol. He squealed with delight and headed for the nearest sink. I was not so pleased. I turned to Mom and said, "I'm surprised at you. Don't you remember how we used to drive you crazy with water guns?"

Mom smiled and then replied, "I remember."

—JIM FLICK (Niles, Ohio) July 1990

I have always fought a tendency to be overprotective of my growing children. Apologetically I would say to my firstborn, "I've never had a son your age before, and I need to be a little older so I can get used to it." This explanation carried us through new experiences in his life that ranged from his first airplane trip alone to getting his driver's license.

Then he left for college, and all my anxieties returned until he called me one day in October. "Rush is starting, Mom," he said fondly. "Are you old enough for me to join a fraternity?"

—JANE H. HARVEY (Greenville, S.C.) Oct. 1988

EN ROUTE

Flying above northern Arizona in a jet, I listened as the captain described points of interest over the loudspeaker. He indicated a giant crater on the ground that was formed by a meteorite thousands of years ago.

A young woman in the row ahead of me looked out the window. She then turned to her companion and exclaimed, "Gee, if it had landed a little farther to the right, it would have hit the highway!"

—WALLY COX (San Antonio, Texas) Jan. 1991

I have a horrible habit of referring to my two daughters by age, rather than by name, when talking to people who don't know them. Glenda answered the door one day when my insurance agent and a handsome young trainee rang the bell. The young fellow watched her without batting an eye as she left the room. To break the ice, the agent commented on our piano and asked if I played. "No," I answered, "but my 16-year-old daughter does."

Glenda overheard, but said nothing. However, when some of her friends dropped in that afternoon, I heard her say, "Come on into the kitchen. I want you to meet my 52-year-old mother."

—MRS. CALVIN T. COCHRAN (Atlanta, Ga.) Jan. 1967

When my husband-to-be and I announced our engagement to our two ten-year-old daughters and five-year-old son by previous marriages, the children were delighted. They immediately began a campaign to have us get married sooner than we had planned.

One night they prepared a meal of leftovers and candy, complete with candles and mood music. "Isn't this romantic?" one daughter piped up hopefully. "Just the five of us."

—JUDY WOMACK (Clinton, Miss.) Oct. 1984

One night after a date with her new boyfriend, my 16-year-old daughter, Emily, rushed into the kitchen to share her news. "Mom, he kissed me!" she announced proudly.

My husband and daughter have always been close, and he had been having a hard time facing the fact that she was growing up. I knew he might not wish to hear of her first kiss. Emily, however, had already told him. I was relieved and touched when she repeated their conversation.

"Dad," she had whispered, "he kissed me."

"Honey," he whispered back, "I don't blame him."

—REBECCA BRAKER (Defiance, Ohio) Apr. 1994

The generation gap quickly became apparent when I tried to discuss marriage with my daughter, who is very career-oriented. "A husband might not tolerate your ambition forever," I pointed out. "He might become concerned about how such total dedication to a job could fit into a successful relationship."

"You don't understand, Dad," my daughter countered. "It's going to be a merger, not a takeover."

—L. C. ELMORE (Portola Valley, Calif.) May 1989

My oldest daughter insisted that her true love speak with me, man to man, about his marriage intentions. She had met him overseas and, while I liked everything I'd heard about him, we'd never been introduced. I'm just old-fashioned enough to believe that parental blessing is still necessary for a truly happy union, so I eagerly anticipated our first face-to-face encounter.

The big meeting was scheduled to take place in my office. At the appointed hour, my daughter walked in with a good-looking but anxious fellow in tow. Before I could say a thing, he dropped to one knee, took my right hand in both of his, gazed earnestly up at me and said, "Will you be my father-in-law?"

I couldn't bless them fast enough.

—CLINT KELLY (Everett, Wash.) Mar. 1995

Aunt Karen is the mother of two high-spirited young girls. When I called her one morning, our conversation was constantly interrupted by the din of kids screaming and chasing each other. "Could you hold on for a moment?" my aunt finally asked, putting down the phone.

Within ten seconds all I could hear was absolute silence. Then, "Okay, I'm back."

"But it's so quiet!" I exclaimed. "You must have complete control over those two."

"Not really," my aunt confessed wearily. "I'm in the closet."

—STEVE BRUNDAGE (Salamanca, N.Y.) Apr. 1989

While on maternity leave, a woman from our office brought in her new bundle of joy. She also had her seven-year-old son with her. Everyone gathered around the baby, and the little boy asked, "Mommy, can I have some money to buy a soda?"

"What do you say?" she said.

Respectfully, the boy replied, "You're thin and beautiful."

The woman reached in her purse and gave her son the money.

—MERCURY NICKSE (Shelton, Conn.) May 1991

In line at the supermarket checkout, I noticed a young mother unloading her cart while trying to keep two unruly little boys under control. It was a losing battle. The boys had reached the hair-pulling stage just about the time she was placing her last items on the counter.

As the checker began ringing up, the woman grabbed one item and tossed it back with the tabloids. I assumed it was to have been a treat for the children until I heard her mutter, "Forget it. I don't even want to know."

Glancing at the rack, I saw that she had discarded a home pregnancy test.

—ROBERT LUNDGREN (Avon, Mass.) Aug. 1992

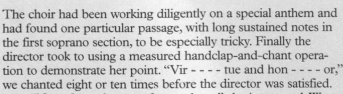

The choir had been working diligently on a special anthem and had found one particular passage, with long sustained notes in the first soprano section, to be especially tricky. Finally the director took to using a measured handclap-and-chant operation to demonstrate her point. "Vir - - - - tue and hon - - - - or," we chanted eight or ten times before the director was satisfied.

"Now, from the top of page three," she instructed. We plunged in—too fast again—only to break up completely at her anguished cry: "Girls! You are not hanging on to your virtue long enough!"

—PAT MOSES (Denver, Colo.) June 1969

While my two-year-old and I were visiting Grandma, the man who delivers hot meals to the elderly came in with her lunch. He complimented me on my son, and then went on to say that he had eight children of his own. "Eight kids!" I exclaimed. "I love my son so much that I can't imagine dividing that love by eight."

"Lady," he said gently, "you don't divide your love. You multiply it."

—KIMBERLEY K. SLUTZ (Bolivar, Ohio) Apr. 1985

FROM THE HEART

Chicago video fans watching station WBKB's "Curbstone Cutup" program usually see half a dozen people interviewed under the marquee of the State-Lake Theater. But one night the entire 15 minutes of the program was devoted to an interview with two little girls, Beverly and Janice Fetzer, aged 13 and 11.

How had the girls spent their summer? Were they helping Mother with the housework? How were they getting on in school?

Television fans couldn't understand why the youngsters were allowed to monopolize the program. A few impatient viewers even called WBKB. What the people of Chicago did not know on that warm summer's night was that for 14 months Joseph Fetzer, father of the girls, had been dying of tuberculosis in an isolation ward of Chicago's Municipal Tuberculosis Sanatorium. And for 14 months he had been prevented from seeing his children by a rigid rule that denied children under 16 entry into an isolation ward.

When Joseph Fetzer knew the end was near he made one last request—that he see his children. He himself suggested television as the only possible way. Officials of Station WBKB agreed at once. And so that was how Joseph Fetzer had one last and loving look at Beverly and Janice—the night before he died.

—S. C. QUINLAN (WBKB, Chicago, Ill.) Jan. 1950

I stopped to chat with an elderly neighbor whose husband had died during the past year. Her daughter and son-in-law were visiting her, and I asked about her plans for the coming months. She expressed her desire to spend a month at her summer home. "After that, she'll probably stay a few months in St. Louis with my sister, and then come back home with me," her daughter interjected.

The older woman smiled lovingly at her daughter. "They tell me what to do, and I do it," she said. "I used to be the mother of four children. Now, it seems, I'm the child of four mothers."

—Mary Matuzak (Flushing, Mich.) Apr. 1986

Our friend, who had just turned 60, was doing some spring planting, with the help of his 91-year-old father. When the older man began to put up beanpoles in straight lines, the son suggested that stacking them tepee-style was better. A disagreement arose.

"Dad," our friend finally said, sighing, "this is *my* garden, and I want to use the tepees."

The father threw down his hoe and stomped off toward the house. "You kids!" he snorted over his shoulder. "Turn sixty and think you know everything!"

—Maggie Wallem Rowe (Hudson, N.H.) May 1986

When Joe Wilson finished college and joined his father in a small family-owned business, Mr. Wilson was overjoyed. "It will be good to have some aggressive young management around the place," he said. "Your first duty as my new partner is to replace that sign out front with one of those father-and-son signs—you know the kind."

"Yes, I know just what we need," Joe said. Later he invited his father out to inspect the new sign.

Mr. Wilson was speechless for a moment. Then he chuckled and said, "Now that's what I call real aggressive young management." The sign read: Joe C. Wilson & Father.

—Max B. Richardson (Woods Cross, Utah) Dec. 1968

ISBN 0-89577-855-6